How to Plan a Small Garden

Publishing Director Laura Bamford
Creative Director Keith Martin
Executive Editor Julian Brown
Editor Karen O'Grady
Senior Designer Geoff Fennell
Design Steve Byrne
Production Controller Julie Hadingham
Picture Research Zoe Holtermann

First published in Great Britain in 1998
by Hamlyn
an imprint of Reed Consumer Books Limited
Michelin House, 81 Fulham Road, London SW3 6RB and
Auckland, Melbourne, Singapore and Toronto

Copyright © 1998 Reed Consumer Books Limited

ISBN 0 600 59429 7

A catalogue record for this book is available from the British Library

Produced by Toppan
Printed in China

How to Plan a Small Garden

Richard Bird

hamlyn

contents

introduction

In the garden, as much effort can be exerted as you wish. Many people will want returns for a minimum amount of effort, while others find that it is the effort as much as the results that they enjoy and so are prepared to work. Like many skills, some are born to it while others have to work hard at it. However, with a little common sense anyone can grow plants, and grow them successfully. There is no reason why anyone should not be able to create a garden to suit them and their family without it costing the earth. The real skill comes in knowing what you want and this is where this book comes in; by helping you to decide.

An attractive outside space can be created with the minium amount of time spent maintaining it. This space would use a maximum amount of hard surface with decoration from artifacts rather than plants. A few trees and shrubs could be added to move it one step nearer to a garden, and these would take very little maintenance. The additional use of containers would begin to make the space look even more like a garden, but still the amount of time spent would be minimal. With more time spent in the garden, the area of hard surfacing could be reduced and the number of borders and the amount of plants increased until you arrive at a situation where perhaps a retired person could spend much of their time tending their plants with great enjoyment. Somewhere in this spectrum lies your ideal. Think carefully about it and work out how much time you can devote to the garden and then match this to the type of garden you would like.

The garden should reflect your own interests and lifestyle. It is not a static object and it can be changed from time to time much in the same manner as house decoration changes, although, plants take a little longer to

settle in than paint does to dry. There are so many different styles from which to chose. Wandering around other gardens, and looking at books will generate ideas as well as your own inventiveness.

One of the main decisions is whether you require a formal or informal look. Gardeners with families will often choose the latter, as will many who want a contrast from their ordered business lives. Others, however, may prefer to have a more ordered, uncluttered garden in which lines are crisp and clear rather than indistinct and understated, as they frequently are in an informal garden. Of course things need not be too clear-cut and a garden can be a blend of the two, or can contain both in separate areas.

The actual size of a garden in many respects is irrelevant; what you do with it is more important. Two people with a small town garden may well treat it in totally different ways, one choosing a minimal approach while another fills the space with literally hundreds of plants. It is surprising what can be done with even the smallest patch.

One of the most important exercises when planning a garden is to sit down and draw up a list of what you need from your garden. The requirements should be ranked in order of priority as there might not be room for them all, or some uses may conflict with others. For example, room for children's games, such as football, is likely to conflict with a desire to have the best manicured lawn in the neighbourhood. On the other hand, thinking ahead, space allocated for games may well be transformed into a dream lawn once the children have grown up.

Once you have worked out what you want, consider whether, realistically, you are going to have the time and money to achieve what you want. It is

very easy to take on more than you can manage and end up with a part finished garden that becomes more of a nightmare than a pleasure.

It is a good idea to draw up a plan, marking in fixed features, such as trees and sheds, that you would like to retain. Also include areas of permanent

Making use of space
The perfect small garden (opposite) with plenty of hard space on which to relax as well as lots of flowering plants in beds, containers and on the walls. All the space is used to the best advantage, and the result is an inviting garden, ideal for relaxing and entertaining friends.

shade and maximum sun, and any other relevant details. Then see if you can fit in what you want to achieve. When you have finished, go out and try to visualise it to see whether it will work. Mark out areas with string or hose pipe and see what it looks like on the ground. Do not start straight away but live with the idea and the plans for a few weeks, looking at the garden in different light and weather to see how it will work. When you are satisfied, it is time to start getting your hands dirty.

Gardening can be very rewarding. It allows you to create a personal space that is not dictated by external pressures, it can be truly yours. It provides good, regular exercise and the opportunity to spend time in the open air. For many, dealing with growing and propagating plants is a fascinating pastime, and here lies one of the main problems, it can become addictive – you have been warned!

Looking at the site

Before you start

To get the best out of a garden it is essential to study its physical presence closely before any work is carried out. Usually one is in a hurry to get on and design the garden, but a period of contemplation will ultimately save a lot of time an energy in correcting wrongly placed features.

Soil conditions?

The acidity of the soil may not be too much of a worry if there are no specific plant requirements, it is just a matter of making certain that the plants you buy will grow on your particular type of soil. Most will, but there is a serious problem if you want to grow acid-loving plants, such as rhododendrons and your soil is alkaline. There is little you can do about this except plant any such plants in a special ericaceous compost in containers. A soil-testing kit can be bought very cheaply from garden centres and will provide a quick analysis of the soil. Most provide a checklist of what is required to redress any deficiencies found.

Too much water?

Waterlogged soil is hopeless for any sort of garden except for growing bog-loving plants. If the soil lays wet, especially if it has puddles on it, it should be drained. It may be possible to drain the water into a feature such as a pond. The alternative is to dig a soak-away (a large hole loosely filled with rubble) and lay land drains to carry the water from the soil into it.

Best beds?

Some parts of the garden may have been used for beds before and may be in better condition that the rest of the garden. These will usually show up as being darker, freer draining, with soil that is easier to dig. It may be sensible to use these areas again if it fits in with the rest of the plan.

Sun and shade?

Sun and shade are important things to consider. Look carefully where the shadows fall and where the best areas of sunlight fall. The latter may be used for patios or places where it would be pleasant to sit in the sun. Flower borders for sun-loving plants should also be allocated to these areas. Shady areas can be used for shade-loving plants as well as areas for sitting during very hot weather. As, on the whole shady areas are not so useful, these are the best places to put dustbins or sheds.

What to keep?

Except in brand-new gardens, there is usually at least something that can be kept. Trees, in particular, should be kept unless there are overwhelming reasons for removing them. Shrubs, beds and lawns may already be in existence, but do not be forced to compromise your plan by their presence. Remove them if need be as it is easy to establish new beds and new plants will quickly grow to replace what was there before. There may be unattractive existing features such as sheds, garages, greenhouses or oil tanks. They can be incorporated into the scheme, making the most of them or it may be possible to remove them completely.

Drawing a plan?

Before starting to consider what to do with the garden it is a good idea to draw up a plan of the existing garden, showing every dimension and the position of all existing features and plantings. Also put in such hindrances as manhole covers and drains. Once this has been done it means that when you sit round the kitchen table discussing or thinking about the new garden, you will be able to accurately see what you have got, both in terms of the space there is to play with and the existing features that may be incorporated.

Time to look around

Finally, just walking round and looking at the garden from all angles, in all lights and, if possible, in all seasons, will often suggest the ideal layout for the garden. Certain features will fit perfectly into certain places and the rest will slip into place around them. The garden will simply begin to appear before your eyes and then all you have to do is to make it happen!

Before starting
- Draw up a list of priorities
- Check soil conditions
- Check sunny and shady areas
- Check access points
- Draw up plan of existing features
- Carry out basic tasks such as checking drainage, installing services, repairing or making fences.

▶▶ Also see: Organic gardening p.46-7, Tool Guide p.122-3

QUES

how to plan

TION

a small garden

NAIRE

Q U E S

What type of garden do you have?

What do you want to do in your garden?

What do you want to have in the garden?

When do you want to be in the garden?

Who will be using the garden?

What style of garden do you want?

These questions are designed to help you assess your lifestyle needs, practical concerns and environmental factors.

Before creating the small garden of your dreams it is essential to plan carefully.

Use each section to discover how to create the ideal small garden for you.

A I R E

What problem areas does my garden have?

What about the children?

Tools and Equipment checklist

☐ Buckets
☐ Chainsaw
☐ Cultivator
☐ Dibber
☐ Fork
☐ Garden line
☐ Gloves
☐ Hand fork
☐ Hedge trimmer
☐ Hoe
☐ Hosepipe
☐ Lawn edger
☐ Lawn aerator
☐ Lawn fertiliser spreader
☐ Lawn mower
☐ Leaf sweepers
☐ Long-arm tree pruners
☐ Loppers
☐ Pruning saw
☐ Rake
☐ Rotavator or mechanical cultivator
☐ Secateurs
☐ Shears
☐ Shredder
☐ Spade
☐ Sprinklers
☐ Strimmer
☐ Trowel
☐ Watering can
☐ Wheelbarrow

What kind of plants do you want to grow in your garden?

What sort of features do you want in your garden?

low maintenance

Less is more

It is possible to get carried away when designing a garden, forgetting just how much work is involved in its maintenance. There is no doubt that the best gardens do need a lot of attention, more than most people can afford to give them, but on the other hand, with careful planning, a very attractive garden can be created that only requires the minimum of effort.

How much time?

Before deciding which type of garden to create it is important to decide how much time can be spent on it and how this time is broken down. If time is limited to a couple of hours at weekends then it is important to design a low maintenance garden, especially as some weekends will be lost through bad weather. If you can spare an hour a day, then the possibilities are much greater and there can be a greater emphasis on time-consuming flowering borders.

To mow or not to mow?

One of the great time-consumers is mowing the lawn. What is the lawn used for? Is it possible to use an alternative?. A hard surface, such as paving or brickwork, needs hardly any attention apart from occasional sweeping. Chipped bark is a much softer surface, softer even than grass and would certainly make a good alternative for play areas.

Hard boundaries?

Similarly, hedges will need to be cut, so use solid fences as a boundary instead. If hedges are preferred, use a slow growing one such as yew, which takes longer to establish but once grown needs only one trim a year.

Who wants weeding?

While some gardeners actually like weeding, to the majority it is not only a great waste of time, but also extremely tedious. Cut this out and a great deal of time is saved. Weedkillers are one alternative but apart from the initial clearing of the ground they are not recommended in an established garden for a wide variety of reasons including safety. The way to combat weeds is to use a mulch. Cover the borders with 10cm (4in) of bark and weed seed will not germinate.

Who wants watering?

Another boring and time consuming job is watering lawns and plants. If you have to water then it is possible to use mechanical devices such as sprinklers, but it is much better to reduce the amount of water required by, once again, mulching. The mulch prevents the water evaporating from the surface of the soil, leaving it in the ground and so available to the plants.

Are there plants to save time?

The choice of plants is important if you want to save time as some plants require more attention than others. For example a fair number of shrubs and most small trees require little if any pruning. Check when buying just how much attention each requires. The same is true of many perennials, some need to be staked, deadheaded and divided at regular intervals, while others seem to thrive on inattention. Again, check when buying.

Small is beautiful

Reduce the amount of garden you have to look after by growing things in pots and other containers. They require more watering than the open borders but need overall less attention and can produce really satisfying results with relatively little effort.

Low maintenance surfaces
Paved areas are much easier to maintain than grass ones. In a small garden, their clear lines and uncluttered surface makes the space seem larger. As well as presenting far less work than a lawn, paving also cuts the cost and storage requirements for machinery and tools to maintain it.

container planting

Using containers is an ideal way of looking after plants in a small garden. It allows much greater flexibility than a conventional border as groupings can be changed regularly. Plants can be kept out of sight until in flower, while dead ones can be removed. A wide range of plants can be used, colourful annuals or leafy perennials, depending on the mood and effect required.

All in miniature
Containers can be used to brighten up areas of a garden or provide different elements of the garden in miniature. Here modern stainless steel pots contain lush grasses, echoing the lawns of larger gardens.

What to use?

Containers can be anything from flowerpots, to urns on pedestals, window boxes or hanging baskets. There is a wide selection, each in a number of materials, available from garden centres. With ingenuity they can be recycled for other uses. Old galvanized buckets and watering cans make splendid containers, but on the other hand large plastic margarine tubs are unattractive to the eye, especially if they have any form of advertising slogan printed on them.

Planting?

If the container is large or heavy, place it in its final position before filling it as it will be very heavy once filled with compost. Place a few small stones in the bottom of the container to help with drainage and then fill with a good compost. Plant the plants at the same depth as they were in their original containers. Water thoroughly.

Maintenance?

It is essential to water containers, regularly – at least once a day in hot dry weather. Feed once a week with a liquid feed added to the water during the summer months. The frequency of watering can be reduced by adding water-retaining granules to the compost at the time of planting. Similarly, a slow-release fertiliser added to the compost will supply nutrients for several months. Both are readily available from garden centres. Move tender and exotic plants under cover for the winter.

Type of Container

	Advantages	Disadvantages
Terracotta	Attractive, relatively lightweight, difficult to over-water	May be damaged by frost, loses moisture fast, may be expensive
Stone	Attractive	Heavy, expensive
Cement	Can be attractive, relatively cheap	May look ugly, heavy
Wood	May be attractive, relatively light, can be home-made	Can rot, needs treating with preservative or paint
Plastic	Inexpensive, lightweight	Often very plain, easy to over-water
Glass-fibre	Attractive reproductions	Expensive
Lead	Very attractive	Very expensive, very heavy

Which annuals and tender perennials?

Ageratum
Alonsoa
Antirrhinum majus
Arctototis stoechadifolia
Argyranthemum
Begonia semperflorens
Bidens ferulifolia
Brachycome iberidifolia
Convolvulus tricolor
Gazania
Helichrysum petiolare
Impatiens
Lobelia erinus
Osteospermum
Pelargonium
Petunia
Plectranthus coleoides
Senecio cinerea
Tagetes
Tropaeolum
Verbena x hybrida
Viola x wittrockiana

Which shrubs?

Acer palmatum 'Dissectum'
Ballota pseudodictamnus
Buxus sempervirens
Callistemon citrinus
Camellia
Convolvulus cneorum
Cordyline australis
Erica
Fuchsia
Hebe
Helianthemum
Hydrangea
Hypericumv
Ilex
Indigofera
Kalmiav
Laurus nobilis
Lavandula
Olearia
Phormium
Pittosporum
Rhododendron
Rosemarinus
Skimmia
Yucca

Which perennials ?

Acanthus mollis
Agapanthus
Begonia x tuberhybrida
Dianthus
Diascia
Euphorbia
Hosta
Phormium
Primula
Sedum
Stachys byzantina

▶▶ Also see: Flower power p.68-9, Under glass p.56-7

Variety

Above: The scope for the use of containers in a small garden is tremendous, both in the shape and nature of the container and in their contents. Be prepared to use unconventional containers or to use conventional containers in unconventional ways. Ingenuity is the key to success.

A fresh face

Left: One advantage of containers is that it is very easy to change the scene. This can be achieved simply by rearranging all the pots within their group. Alternatively the pots can be regrouped in other parts of the garden. A third possibility is to introduce new containers as their flowers come into bloom.

general low maintenance

Weeds in paving
If paving slabs are laid in the conventional way on sand without cement joints, then weeds will constantly appear between them. Laying down a black polythene membrane first will prevent weeds coming up from the underlying soil. Cementing the joints between slabs will also avoid this, as well as preventing fresh weed seed slipping in-between the slabs.

As well as choosing a design of garden and plants that are low maintenance, there are also techniques that help to keep the amount of work to a minimum.

The key to success?
There are two important things to remember in order to keep the work load down – thorough preparation, and little and often.

Thorough preparation?
If everything is well prepared then there is less likely to go wrong. Make certain, for example that all perennial weeds have been removed before any planting takes place as they will be at least twice as difficult to remove once plants are growing. Similarly plenty of well-rotted organic material added to the soil when the beds are prepared will not only help to condition the soil, but will also supply nutrients and will hold moisture down near the plant's roots, reducing the amount of feeding and watering required over several seasons.

Little and often?
If the amount of work is allowed to get on top it can be a long slog to regain control. If weeds are plucked out when they are seen, they are easy to control, but if they are allowed to grow away they soon get in amongst the plants and are very difficult to remove. A relaxing stroll round the garden every evening, removing any weed that has dared emerge during the day will save many hours work at a weekend, when there are likely to be many more important things to do. Similarly, catching pests at an early stage in their development will not only save time later on, but will also give the plants a better chance of survival in top condition.

Mulches?
Use mulches to reduce the amount of watering and to prevent weeds germinating. However before laying down a mulch remove perennial weeds as a mulch will not prevent these reappearing. Similarly water the ground thoroughly before applying the mulch. Always top up when it begins to wear thin.

Ground cover?
Ground cover plants will also help to reduce the amount of weeding, but, again, they will not prevent perennial weeds that are already in the soil from growing. Remove every piece before planting the ground cover.

Staking?
Staking perennial plants that need staking takes time, choose plants that do not flop over at the first breath of wind. If some plants are at risk, stake them early, before they are half grown as this is much easier than waiting until they are either fully grown or have already fallen over.

Mulches

	Advantages	Disadvantages
Chipped bark	Looks natural in most positions	Some of the bigger chips can look ugly
Black polythene	Cheap, very efficient	Unsightly
Leaf-mould	Very natural, excellent soil conditioner	Not readily available unless home made
Gravel	Attractive	Not suitable for all borders, becomes mixed into the earth and needs constant renewing
Spent mushroom compost	Excellent soil conditioner	No good near acid-loving plants as it contains chalk
Farmyard manure	Excellent soil conditioner	Must not be used fresh, may contain weed seed
Grass cuttings	Readily available. Best used at back of borders	Unsightly, must not be used in too deep a layer

 ▶▶ Also see: Quick tricks p.60-1, Container planting p.12-3

Living mulch
While plants must be given enough space to thrive, planting them as close together as possible reduces the amount of weeds that will grow in a bed or border. In effect the plants create a living mulch or a ground cover.

Evening stroll
Plants are kept in a much better condition and are much easier to look after if they are attended to regularly. A five minute relaxing stroll around them every evening, will save hours of intensive work at some later stage.

Ground cover plants
Aegopodium
Asarum
Asperula
Aucuba
Brunnera
Carex
Claytonia
Convallaria
Cornus canadensis
Dryopteris
Epimedium
Euonymus fortunei
Euonymus japonicus
Euphorbia amygdaloides robbiae
Gaultheria
Hedera
Hosta
Lamium
Lysimachia nummularia
Maianthemum
Pachysandra
Pulmonaria
Rhododendron
Sarcococca
Tiarella
Vaccineum
Vancouveria
Vinca

entertaining

Making the most of sunny days and warm evenings

One of the most delightful ways of using outside space is to share it with others. Entertaining guests during a warm summer's evening or a sunny lunch time is one of the great joys in life. To do it successfully, in a relaxing attractive atmosphere that you have created yourself, makes doubly so.

Location

There are three aspects to entertaining outside. The first is simply standing around talking with drinks, the second is similar except the participants are seated, and the third sitting down for a meal. It is the last that requires the most thought. If possible, site the area you wish to use near the house, so that access is simple, especially to the kitchen.

On the other hand if the area immediately next to the house is in constant shade, it may be better to locate it where there is some sun, even if you modify it to a dappled shade. Avoid windy positions, especially those where gaps between buildings cause vortices of wind even on still days. Another thing to avoid is dustbins. They should be out of sight and certainly not within smelling distance.

Enough Space?

The size of the area may well depend on what space there is in the garden, but if possible it ought to be tailored to your lifestyle. For dinners a deux then a small arbour will not only suffice but will present the right kind of atmosphere. On the other hand most people will want to have space for a table that seats at least four, which will involve an absolute minimum area of 2x2m(6ft7in). A larger area can be reduced to a more intimate setting by adding or moving containers of plants.

In the shade?

Shade is an important aspect to consider. Some people may like to entertain in full sun, but most prefer, at least to eat in shade. Shade can be provided as a permanent feature or a removable one. From the temporary point of view it can simply be created by one or more parasols. On a more lavish scale an awning can be erected on poles or pulled out from a more permanent fixing on a wall. The design of these can be in subdued, oatmeal colour or more gay stripes or multicolours.

A more rural atmosphere can be provided by creating shade with plants. This can be from a tree or large shrub, or from climbers draped over a framework. Grape vines are extremely good in this respect as they supply a wonderful dapple shade, that is ideal for eating under.

Barbecue?

Depending on the type and scale of the entertaining, it may be desirable to include a barbecue in the area. This can be a permanent, built-in feature, or a mobile one stored elsewhere (see page 20). Evening entertaining is likely to go on beyond nightfall and some additional kind of lighting may be required. While candles create a romantic atmosphere, electric lighting may also be required, so it is worth considering laying a permanent power line to the area concerned.

Plants?

Planting in an entertaining area is a matter of choice. Fragrant climbing and other plants help to create a relaxing atmosphere, while foliage plants help to create a cool, restful ambience as well as privacy. Flowers add a touch of gaiety or romance depending on their colours. Whites and blues show up best in evening light.

Breakfast al fresco
Being able to dine outside whenever the weather permits is one of the great advantages of developing your own garden. Plants create the ideal surroundings for al fresco eating, whether it is a quick meal after work or a more relaxed supper party. The constantly changing vegetation and flowers makes the backdrop more varied and interesting than an indoor room, while the outside summer air cannot be reproduced within a house or flat.

barbecues

Undoubtedly one of the most popular activities in the garden today is that of holding a barbecue. With portable barbecues and a wide range of cooking materials so readily available and easy to use, it has become a universal way of entertaining family and friends.

Permanent or portable?

There are three types of barbecue. A built-in one which is a permanent structure, a portable one that can be moved around the garden, and a hybrid of the two; one made from bricks or concrete blocks that are dry jointed and so can be dismantled and rebuilt elsewhere should the mood take. Built-in barbecues can be part of the structure of one area of the garden, with low walls or built-in benches to sit on, as well as tables and storage facilities, all being part of the complex. A chimney helps to funnel the smoke and smells away.

Where do you place it?

Siting should be considered carefully. While it is convenient to be close to the house and the kitchen, cooking smells and smoke may annoy neighbours, so it is often better to locate it as far away as possible. Mobile barbecues have the advantage that you can move them to a position where smoke and smells do not blow over your guests or aggravate neighbours. Avoid siting the barbecue too near plants, fences or buildings that may scorch or even catch light. Keep a fire-blanket and water near at hand, just in case.

Make certain there is enough room for all the guests, barbecues generally take up more room than a more sedentary meal as there are frequently more guests and they often move about rather than sit round a table. While it can take place on a lawn, a hard stand is preferable, at least for location of the barbecue itself. It is easier to clean and will take the constant trampling better than grass, especially if there has been recent rain.

Brick built
Opposite: A built-in barbecue can be a simple structure, as here, or can be part of a larger complex that includes, built-in benches, tables and even storage facilities. Home-made barbecues usually burn charcoal. Leave plenty of room around the barbecue, but if, as here, space is limited, serve the food away from the barbecue.

Portable
Right: A portable barbecue does not fit into the garden as well as a built-in one, but it is much more versatile. It can be moved to different areas, depending on the weather, and can be put out of sight when not in use. Although you can buy elaborate, expensive models, a very basic portable can be purchased very cheaply. Small, tray-like portable barbecues can be used as the working parts inside a built-in structure.

Fuels

	Advantages	Disadvantages
Charcoal	Traditional barbecue fuel easily available, fun	Need to wait at least 30 minutes for the right heat. Can burn out
Gas	Easy, clean, no waiting	Not so much fun as creating your own fire
Wood	Traditional camp-fire material. Readily available	Not easy to get hot enough with small fire. smoke and soot taints the food

  ▶▶ Also see: Disguising essentials p.112-3

Gas-fired
A modern gas-fired barbecue is one of the easiest and cleanest to operate, but lacks some of the primitive fun of lighting one's own fire. They are run from gas cylinders and can therefore be located anywhere in the garden. Although they can be built-in they are usually mobile. They should be stored under cover.

Siting barbecues
- Avoid annoying neighbours and guests with smoke and smells
- After other considerations, place as near to kitchen as possible
- Avoid drafty positions
- Avoid scorching plants, fences and buildings
- Allow plenty of space round the barbecue
- Preferably have a hard surface around the barbecue
- Mobile units allow you to position the barbecue according to conditions and require

Building a barbecue
- Ensure it is well sited
- Make certain structure is stable
- Build it high enough to avoid bending
- Allow enough grilling space
- Allow variable heights for cooking grills
- Build up the wall above the grills to act as a windshield
- If possible build the walls up to form a chimney to funnel smoke away
- Include space for tools, condiments, cooked and uncooked food
- Plant herbs nearby

Safety
- Make certain that the barbecue is stable
- Keep away from inflammable materials such as wooden fences
- Avoid damaging shrubs and other plants
- Keep children and pets under control
- Have fire-blanket and water to hand
- The cook should not over-imbibe

furniture

Furniture for the garden should be chosen just as carefully as furniture for the house. It should fit in with the overall appearance of the garden as well as having qualities such as comfort and ease of maintenance. If there are children around, it should be strong enough to take some abuse or alternatively be cheap enough to be replaced. furniture can be very expensive and so the financial aspects should be considered carefully.

Stylish seating
A simple wooden bench that is the ideal size for a small garden. It has an eloquence about it that makes it a decorative feature in the garden as well as a practical one for sitting upon If wood, regular maintenance will be required to keep the bench in good condition. If plastic, apart from an occasional wipe down no regular maintenance is required.

Comfort?
Most seating benefits from cushions. These not only add to the comfort but also add colour. Some are made in such a way that they can be left outside during the summer, but most are best kept inside when not in use. In many small gardens there is little chance to move around and seating or tables can be built in as part of the a patio area.

Strength?
The weight of furniture is important, some, stone in particular is so heavy that it needs to be left permanently in place, while others, such as aluminium framed chairs, can easily be moved around to follow the sun or the shade.

Always consider the amount of maintenance required. Some furniture needs more than others, especially if it is to be left permanently outside.

Cheap furniture
A simple, cheap seat can be built by bolting a plank of wood across two brick piers or supporting it on two sections of tree-trunk

Seats – benches or individual?
The most basic furniture is seating, consisting of benches or individual seats. They can be heavy if permanently positioned, but need to be lighter around tables. If you intend to eat or take drinks outside then a table is essential. There is a large range of sizes available. For sun bathing or relaxing a whole range of loungers, swinging seats and hammocks can be purchased. Swing seats come with their own framework but hammocks need secure fixing on trees or in walls. Folding furniture, such as director's chairs, are a great advantage in a small garden, but it does need somewhere to be stored. Sunshades and parasols are also important features of garden furniture.

Materials

	Advantages	Disadvantages
Wood	Usually looks good, can be folding, can be painted, can be custom or home built	Cheap items can become loose and unstable, needs maintaining, needs covering or storing in winter. Some woods last longer than others
Plastic	Cheap, little maintenance, lightweight, usually comfortable. Can be folding	Limited colour range, looks like plastic, needs covering or storing in winter
Steel and cast alloys	Solid, long lasting, can be good looking. Can be painted	Cold and hard without cushions, can rust if not maintained
Aluminium	Cheap, little maintenance, lightweight. Can be folding	Frequently looks cheap, fabric seats and backs not long lasting, can become unstable. Those with fabric need storing when not in use
Stone or reproduction stone	Heavy, looks permanent, usually blends in well, easy to maintain	Cold, hard, cannot be moved. May need solid foundation
Fabrics	Wide range of colours, lightweight	Need to be stored when not in use

▶▶ Also see: Illuminating the garden p.28-9, Barbecues p.18-9

Dining out

Above: Breakfast, lunch, evening meal or just a cup of coffee. a small space is required for a table and a couple of chairs and you have the setting for a few minutes or even hours of relaxation in the fresh air.

Sunny Days

Left: The use of this slatted wooden lounger is a perfect way to relax. It is relatively light and can easily be moved around, although it will need some maintenance to keep its appearance fresh. Although shaped, the wood may become hard for prolonged lounging and more cushions may be required.

Keypoints

Appearance
Comfort
Cost
Maintenance
Weight
Strength
Storage
requirements

fun & games

Temporary games

Badminton
Croquet
French cricket
Frisbee
Pole tennis
Skittles
Volley ball

So often gardens can become serious places, where the sole purpose seems to be to act as custodian to a collection of plants. However, nothing can be more satisfying on a sunny afternoon or a warm evening than having a relaxed, pleasurable time with a few friends. This may be simply sitting around enjoying food and conversation, or include activities and games.

Nets and hoops?

Some games need little more than a lawn and can be brought out and set up whenever they are needed. A scratch game of badminton can be played over a temporary net on any rectangular lawn. The quality of the grass surface is immaterial. Croquet is another game that can give immense pleasure but requires little other than a smooth lawn (even a few bumps should not matter as it will be the same for everybody playing). The great thing about these games is that the lawn can be cleared and another, different game played.

Through the hoop
Croquet was once the province of the rich with large gardens and immaculate lawns. It is increasingly being enjoyed by people with much smaller gardens even if it does mean bending the rules a bit to fit the size and shape of the lawn.

Mazes?

Some people have a love of particular games that require more of a permanent set up. Clock golf, for example, may need one or more holes in the lawn, but others may be far more elaborate. Having great aesthetic appeal as well as being fun are mazes. These may be created two-dimensionally on the ground, simply by mowing the grass in a pattern, or by using different coloured bricks. Although they can be three-dimensional, these are more difficult to fit into a small garden as they require hedges.

Swimming?

A swimming pool is something that many people would dearly love to own. It is possible to have one in a small garden, either a properly constructed one, sunk into the ground, or a less expensive one raised above. The latter often comes in kit form and can be erected by the owner, but the proper pools are much more complicated and are best built by professionals. If there are children around, consider the safety implications carefully.

Relax or work out
There is plenty of scope in a small garden for games and sport of all sort. A patio can provide the ideal site for setting up table tennis (top), while guest, old and young will enjoy a decorative maze laid in stone or grass (above). If finances allow it, even a swimming pool (left) can be constructed in all but the smallest of gardens.

romantic images

Hearts and flowers

So often gardens look like a bomb-site rather than a haven of peace and quiet. But there is no reason why this should be so, a little thought and the correct choice of plants can turn even the most barren of sites into a romantic haven. a place for amorous encounters or simply a place to relax after a day's work.

The right atmosphere?

The mood of a garden is important, and one of the most popular is that which appeals directly to the romantic senses. Plants are mainly responsible for creating this atmosphere but it also depends on the structures, summerhouses, arbours and the like. In the evening as the sun begins to set, it is important to choose your method of lighting carefully as, it can create the perfect mood for sitting or strolling.

Privacy?

The romantic garden needs to be private. It is particularly important to create boundaries using trees, shrubs, hedges or even fences to achieve this. This is not so much to stop prying eyes as to create an atmosphere of intimacy. The garden should ideally consist of winding paths and individual areas cut off from one another by plants.

Colour?

The colours in a romantic garden are of great importance; bright hot colours are not for this garden, except for occasional splashes. Soft pastel colours paint a more ethereal picture. It is their misty quality with colours merging that create the desired atmosphere.

Fragrance?

As well as colour, fragrance is one of the most desirable qualities in plants. This is certainly true of the romantic garden. Plenty of scented flowers and foliage through which the fingers can run gives a garden a quality all of its own. Strongly scented paths along the drive or by the gate give a place a strong identity when people arrive.

Bowers?

There must be plenty of places to sit and soak up the atmosphere in a romantic garden. Seats should be dotted around, some of which should be tucked away amidst shrubs or in arbours that are surrounded by climbing plants. Again, as many of the plants as possible should be fragrant. If possible the bowers should be big enough to accommodate a table as well as seating, allowing meals to be taken in them.

Fixtures and fittings?

The permanent garden furniture should not be plain or make-shift; it should fit in with the style of the garden. Wrought or cast iron furniture made to Victorian or Edwardian designs are perfect as is stone furniture. Stone or reproduction-stone statuary also adds to the scene when placed in the right settings. These may be at focal points at the end of a bend in a path, or peering from behind foliage. Stone urns are also very effective.

Water?

Water also adds its magical qualities to a romantic garden. Water can be full of reflections and sounds, which can be heard even if not seen. Even a small pool can be charming. Areas around pools are often damp, forming the perfect situation for the large-leaved plants that love these conditions. These areas of dense foliage bring a certain gothic quality to the mood of the scene.

Setting the scene
With surprisingly little effort it is easy to turn a garden into a romantic setting in which to entertain or relax. Whether it is for two or more (or even simply for personal relaxation and enjoyment), a few fragrant plants and the right illumination will transform a garden or patio on a warm summer's evening.

romantic planting

One of the keys to a romantic garden is good, imaginative planting. The smell of fragrant plants, their soft colours and the hum of contented bees as they go about their business all contribute to the atmosphere, and help to create a haven of tranquillity and calm.

Sweeping beds?

There may well not be much room in a small garden for sweeping beds of flowers, but with a bit of ingenuity a good attempt can be made. One trick is to curve the borders so that they disappear out of sight behind other features, giving the impression that they go on for much further than they actually do. Use a wide range of plants that come into flower from spring to autumn to provide continuity. Soft, pastel colours are the most romantic, and also have the advantage of receding from the eye, making the beds look larger. A solid block of colour, such as a hedge, behind the beds is best for setting off the colour of the flowers. Incorporate as many butterfly plants, such as buddleja, as possible as these add to the atmosphere. The drone of bees is very atmospheric so add plenty of flowering plants for them to enjoy. Use the sunny side of the garden for these beds.

Rambling climbers?

Great swags of roses or honeysuckle, particularly the scented varieties, add greatly to the atmosphere. These can be coiled round places to sit, such as bowers or arbours, or can be trained up poles, trellising, along ropes or up through trees.

Nature's scents
One of the most evocative aspects of any garden is the scents it produces. Everything from the fragrance of flowers and foliage to the fresh sweet smell of mown grass and musky smell of decaying leaves all add to the atmosphere that lingers in the mind. Lavender, seen here lining a path, is one of the most evocative of all plant smells.

Overgrown gardens?

Overgrown gardens have a romantic quality about them. However it is better to have a controlled overgrown garden than simply letting one get out of control. The latter will soon decay and become anything but romantic. Use plenty of foliage plants, such as hostas and ferns, as well as dense trees and shrubs. The shadier, damper part of the garden can be used for this type of planting.

Planting for the evening

The summer evening is a special time, and one when many people like to relax in their gardens. Many plants are at their most fragrant at this time of day and should be planted near siting positions. White flowers show up more than any others as the light begins to fade and should be planted where they make maximum impact.

▶ ▶ Also see: Bedding plants p.70-1, Exotic plants p.58-9

White flowers

Achillea ptarmica 'The Pearl'
Amelanchier
Anaphalis margaritacea
Anemone x hybrida 'Honorine
   Jobert
Anthemis punctata cupaniana
Arabis
Argyranthemum frutescens
Aster novae-angliae 'Herbstschnee'
Astilbe 'Irrlicht'
Bellis
Camellia 'Swan Lake'
Campanula latiloba alba
Centranthus ruber albus
Cerastium tomentosum
Choisya ternata
Chrysanthemum
Clematis 'Marie Boisselot'
Convallaria majalis
Convolvulus cneorum
Crambe cordifolia
Dianthus
Digitalis purpurea 'Alba'
Epilobium angustifolium 'Album'
Erica
Eucryphia
Galanthus
Geranium
Gypsophila
Hebe salicifolius
Hydrangea
Iberis sempervirens
Iris
Jasminum
Lamium maculatum 'White Nancy'
Lathyrus
Leucanthemum
Lilium
Lychnis coronaria 'Alba'
Magnolia
Malva moschata alba
Myrrhis odorata
Nicotiana sylvestris
Olearia
Osmanthus
Osteospermum
Paeonia
Penstemon
Petunia
Philadelphus
Phlox
Physostegia virginiana 'Alba'
Polygonatum x hybridum
Prunus
Pulmonaria 'Sissinghurst White'
Rhododendron
Rosa
Smilacina
Spiraea 'Arguta'
Syringa vulgaris 'Albus'
Tulipa
Viola
Zantedeschia aethiopica

Fragrant flowers and foliage

Azara
Berberis x stenophyla
Choisya ternata
Chrysanthemum
Clethra
Convallaria
Corylopsis
Crambe
Daphne
Dianthus
Elaeagnus
Erysimum
Galanthus
Hamamelis
Hesperis
Hyacinthoides
Itea
Laurus nobilis
Lavandula
Lonicera
Lupinus
Magnolia
Mahonia
Monarda
Myrtus
Oenothera
Osmanthus
Philadelphus
Phlox
Primula
Rhododendron luteum
Rosa
Rosmarinus
Santolina
Sarcococca
Skimmia
Viburnum
Viola

Nature's beauty
What better setting can there be for a romantic tryst than that of a garden full of flowers? Even the small plot can contain at least a few flowers, in small beds, in containers or growing up walls or fences. Some flowers are undoubtedly more romantic than others. In the spring camellias (left) must head the list, while roses more than hold their own in the summer.

illuminating the garden

Right lights
Carefully chosen lighting enhances the atmosphere of the garden. Glaring and overall lighting, on the other hand can be unsubtle and often flatten its appearance. There is a very large range of lighting, both with naked flames and electricity, that can be used to flatter your garden and create the right atmosphere.

For many it is the evening when the garden is at its most relaxing, particularly after a day's work. Carefully chosen lighting can effectively enhance the mood. Of course, lighting is also essential for security and seeing one's way about.

Reasons for illuminating the garden include:
- Seeing your way around
- Security concerns
- The magical effect of lighting plants
- Localised lighting for eating or sitting

Blanket cover?
The easiest, but the most boring, is to have blanket cover from a lamp placed high on a building or post so that it completely illuminates the area below it. A much more subtle approach is to have a series of individual lamps where ever they are needed, along the path or drive, beside steps, near sitting areas. There is a whole range of possibilities with posts, bollards and other types of fittings to suit individual styles of garden. Creating shadow is as important as lighting other areas. Only illuminate the areas that really need it.

Flood-lighting?
The same principle applies to illuminating for effect. Do not light all the trees, shrubs and other plants with one even spread. Use several lamps, and remember when placing them that shade effects are as important as the illuminated areas.

On/off?
There is no need for lights to be on permanently, time switches can be used with flood lighting. Infra red switches that detect movement can be used to switch lights on and off on paths and drives. Only having lights on when they are needed not only saves electricity but also reduces light pollution.

Temporary lighting?
It is possible to install temporary lighting for a particular event. As this will usually involve having cables draped around, special low-voltage lighting is to be recommended. These come in many forms including lanterns for hanging and pedestal units for sticking into the ground along paths or round the edge of a patio.

  ▶ ▶ Also see: Entertaining p.16-7

Real flames?

Temporary garden illumination need not be restricted to electric lighting. Candles, flaming torches and paraffin (kerosene) lamps are much softer and have a somewhat magical quality. Flaming torches are particularly good for parties.

Underwater illumination?

Ponds and fountains can look spectacular when lit, especially from below the water. However, special lighting is required, and it must be safely installed.

Safety
- Only use special outside lighting equipment
- Use the correct cabling
- Professionally install equipment
- Check regularly for wear or faults
- Keep naked flames away from inflammable material

young children

Young at heart
When couples with children contemplate designing their first garden, like the rest of the house, it must reflect their needs and habits. Pristine borders and manicured lawns will have to wait until they grow up, unless they are ruled with a rod of iron and not allowed to play.

Perfect place?
A garden is the perfect place for young children. It can provide a secure environment where they can play safely in the fresh air. It allows them to develop all kinds of motive skills from riding bicycles to climbing trees, all under the watchful eye of their parents, and it can leave them with an undying love of gardens and plants, something to enjoy for the rest of their lives.

Designing for children?
Children will want to play ball, dig holes and build camps, and so it is best to accept this and design the garden accordingly. Large open spaces for football, trees for climbing, shrubs for hiding are all part of the fun. Many children like to have things built for them, especially when young. Sand pits, tree-houses and supervised paddling pools are always welcome.

No-go areas?
As long as there is plenty of space that children can use, there is no need to turn the whole garden over to them. Leave room for flower borders and areas for adults to relax in comfort, but learn to live with the occasional ball breaking off flowers or a bicycle accidentally mowing down a shrub. Romantic gardens in particular remain in children's. The fragrance and colour of so many plants are associated with childhood for many adults who grew up in well-designed gardens, so make the garden resemble a garden, rather than a war-zone.

Involve them?
While many basic things, such as swings and sand pits do not change, each generation has its own idea of fun and parents, regretfully, are now a long way from childhood. So when designing and building things for the children, let them get involved rather than confronting them with a perfect play area that you would have liked some 20 or 30 years ago.

Young gardeners?
As well as providing youngsters with somewhere to play safely, a well-designed and well-used garden will also instill a love of gardens. One way to intensify this is to help young children to create their own garden. Attention span and lack of interest in boring jobs often means that the parent will have to do a lot of it, but none-the-less it is something worth doing. Just a small plot will do. Annual flowers and vegetables make the most interesting subjects as something is always happening in the cycle from germination to dying back, whereas shrubs can be rather boring as nothing much happens throughout the year except possibly flowering. Some seed merchants provide seed especially packeted for the needs of children.

Fleeing the nest?
Children are not children forever. When planning the garden try to think to the future as well as the present. For example when designing a sand pit, design it in such a way that it may be converted into a pool at a later stage. Site the lawns that are to be used for play, where you eventually envisage having a lawn with better quality grass. Plant trees and shrubs so that they will mature by the time you get your garden back, giving you a good framework in which to make further plans.

House in the trees
Creating the right atmosphere in which a child's mind can roam and invent is an important part of their development. What better way than creating a tree house? In their own secluded world away from parents, the garden will forever remain in their memories. Once they have left the nest, the adults can take it over for their own use.

safety and security

Sensible precautions
In their search for new experiences, children are often oblivious to danger. It is important to ensure that all gates are firmly latched or even locked to prevent this happening. Dangers from within can include falling from play equipment onto hard surfaces. The blow can be softened by using loose bark to break the fall.

While it is easy to be over-protective with children, their welfare and security are your first priority. There are obvious dangers in a garden that should be eliminated both for the sake of the children and for their parent's peace of mind.

Keep them in?

On of the most important aspects of child safety in the garden, is to make sure that they stay there. An unseen child wandering onto a road or even away from the house is prone to all kind of accidents and problems. Make certain that the garden is surrounded by an adequate boundary of some sort and that all gates are firmly shut and locked with child-proof or out-of-reach catches.

Check to make certain that a child cannot slip through the bars of a gate or fence. Make certain that the arrangements are such that visitors such as postmen or dustmen do not leave open gates that are directly connected to the children's area.

Hard surfaces?

While children need hard surfaces for certain types of games, especially during the winter, it is a good idea to use soft surfaces where they are likely to fall. For example chipped bark can be used to cushion accidental falls from climbing frames or swings.

Out of sight out of mind?

Although they may not be the most beautiful of sights, place the play areas for young children where they can be seen. As children get older and more able to care for themselves, they prefer to have areas of the garden that are secret and away from adults.

Who wants a sweet?

Many plants are poisonous and should be avoided. The berries of many of these can look like sweets to children and can be easily eaten. Even the roots of some poisonous plants, such as Aconitum, may look like potatoes and be eaten during a game. There are plenty of plants that are safe to use so avoid those that are not. While not poisonous, some others can cause harm by stinging or through prickles.

Avoid:

Aconitum	Mantegazzianu
Arum	Laburnum
Colchicum	Ligustrum
Daphne	Rhamnus
Datura	Ruta
Digitalis	Solanum
Euphorbia	Taxus
Heracleum	Wisteria

Water

Water features in a garden must be considered carefully as far as children are concerned. It is important to remember that it is possible to drown in even a few inches of water. If you want to use water, use fountains or spouts whose water disappears between stones into an underground reservoir, so that there is no standing water to cause problems. If there is already a pond make certain that it is securely fenced off or covered over when there are children around.

Glass?

Most gardens contain glass somewhere; perhaps a greenhouse or a coldframe or cloches. Although not particularly satisfactory from the horticultural point of view glass can be replaced by plastic, which is much safer. Alternatively, any areas containing glass can be fenced off. Another real danger can come from children falling onto the unprotected tops of canes, sticks or any other pointed object.

Points to watch for young children
- open gates
- broken fences
- unprotected water
- poisonous plants
- glass
- hidden parts of the garden
- canes and pointed objects

Pond life
One of the greatest dangers in a garden is water. Children are naturally fascinated and drawn to it. All ponds should be securely fenced off or strongly covered in some way. One way of using water but avoiding its problems is to use a bubble fountain.

activities

Swings and sandpits
Right: Swings and ropes are among the most fundamental of childrens play-things. They are readily available in a variety of materials, or can be home made. It is important to make certain that they are secure as children are likely to test them to their limits. The sand pit (below) is another simple plaything that will give hours of pleasure.

Children will always invent their own games, but it is frequently up to adults to provide the right environment for this to happen. This usually means supplying just a few basic things and letting the children work out the detail. Lawns for play, bushes for hiding, trees for climbing are the basics, and can provide hours of fun.

Playtime

As well as just lounging around in gardens, there are plenty of activities that children like to undertake. Many are best left to their own devising, especially when they get a bit older, but there are still many things that can be done that will be appreciated.

Lawns?

One thing that will certainly be needed is a flat lawn. It is likely to get hard wear, so it is no use using fine grasses as play will soon produce bald patches. Use tough grasses that can tolerate running feet.

Hard wearing grasses used singly or in mixtures:

Axonopus – for warmer climates
Eremochloa ophiuroides – for warmer climates
Lolium perenne – for cooler climates
Paspalum notatum – for warmer climates
Poa pratensis – for cooler climates

Sand pits?

For very young children, sand is a fascinating material and a sand pit can give them hours of fun. Site the pit in a position where it can be used for a pool or some other feature when the children grow up. It can be constructed of wood, but should be free from splinters. Special sand can be bought that is suitable for play without staining clothes or containing sharp flints.

Climbing apparatus?

Climbing provides healthy exercise as well as developing self assurance and motif skills. A bought or home-made climbing frame can be provided. It is essential that it is safely constructed and secure in the ground. Swings are also an eternal source of pleasure. Covering the ground with a 10cm (4in) layer of chipped bark will help soften in falls.

Secrets?

Most children love to have secret hideaways in a garden. Thick bushes and screened off areas help to provide this. Even the smallest garden can have its secrets tucked away somewhere.

Tree-houses

Tree-houses are as much fun for adults as they are for children. Older children can build their own, but it usually falls to the parents to help. Safety is, of course, of paramount importance. Since tree-houses may be seen from neighbouring properties, you may need to get planning permission to erect one in some areas. For younger children play-houses on the ground are a great source of fun. Plastic ones can be bought but there is more fun to be had out of a tailor-made one in wood, especially if the children help build it.

Adventure
Climbing frames are not only great fun for children but help to develop many of their motive skills, balance not being the least of them. All frames should be very strongly made and secure in the ground. Timber should not only be strong but free from splinters. Let the children help design and build it.

year-round interest

Making the most of it?

Most people use their gardens only during the summer months, but there is
no reason why they should not be used throughout the year, not necessarily for
sitting in, although even that is possible in some areas, but at least for providing
colour and things of interest. A walk round a garden covered in hoar frost or
snow can be a magical experience.

Plants for all seasons?

With a bit of careful planning it is possible to provide colour in the garden all year round. There
is, obviously, not so much in the winter, but it is surprising how many plants that do flower at
that time of year, many having the added bonus of being fragrant. Even if they do not flower
many trees and shrubs have colourful bark that shows up at this time of year as there are no
leaves to mask it.

Structure?

In summer when everything is grown to its full height the garden is very three-dimensional.
The varying heights not only add interest to the picture but they also mask or allow mere
glimpses of what lies beyond, thus adding an element of intrigue into the design. In winter
much dies back to ground level and the garden can become very flat, especially if the planting
relies mainly on annuals and herbaceous perennials. A few evergreen shrubs or even the naked
stems of deciduous shrubs make all the difference.

Keeping it beautiful?

Do not neglect the garden throughout the summer and autumn. Remove any dead flowers and
stems that are dying back, partly to keep the garden neat and tidy and partly so that the plants
that are in flower show up to their best advantage. This is particularly important during times
when there is not too much actually in flower.

Dead beautiful?

While it is a good thing to remove dead and dying material during the summer months, as the
main flowering seasons come to an end in autumn it does no harm to leave some of the dead
stems and seed heads for winter decoration. The brown stems not only look attractive when
there is nothing else about, but also provide food by way of seeds and sheltering insects for
many birds.

Self-contained?

One way of ensuring colour in the garden all year round is to use containers of some sort,
tubs, window boxes or hanging baskets. Most of the annual and tender plants used in summer
have a very long season and fill most of the time between the end of one year's frosts and the
start of the next. Between this period there are various hardy plants, such as winter pansies,
which will give a continuous display.

Surfaces?

While lawns and grass paths are fine for dry weather, they are not much use during wet
seasons. Hard surfaces are much more practical, especially for paths in constant use. Areas
immediately outside the house are particularly prone to wear and this makes an ideal place
for a hard surfaced patio. It is important to retain grass then a series of stepping stones will
ease the wear when it is wet. Another compromise is to use gravel which is not so hard in
appearance as stone slabs or bricks.

Winter sunshine
Winter is the most difficult
time in the garden, although
with skill, even the smallest
garden can produce flowers
to brighten the dull months.
Winter aconites (*Eranthis
hyemalis*) are the harbingers
of spring. Once their golden
goblets open, it is a sign that
the warmer weather is not
too far away.

seasonal plants and shrubs

Heady days
There is little more evocative of the heady days of summer than flowers that once bloomed in meadows and fields. It is possible to recreate this in a border, as here, with a mixture of corn marigolds (*Chrysanthemum segetum*), poppies (*Papaver rhoeas*), chamomile (*Chamaemelum nobile*) and corn flowers (*Centaurea cyanus*).

There is nothing more satisfying than creating an interesting and colourful garden, particularly one that is of appeal throughout the year. Skillful use of plants and shrubs with different seasons of flowering, and attractive foliage can help to ensure this, making the garden a place of ever-changing beauty.

Mix and match?

Mix the plants together in the borders so that there is always something going on. If winter plants are allocated to one area then that will become dull for the rest of the year.

Spring bulb?

Spring bulbs always have a very fresh appeal that is appropriate to the time of year. On the whole they flower early and then die back for the rest of the year. This makes them ideal for planting amongst shrubs and herbaceous plants which will grow up and cover the spaces where the bulbs have flowered.

Blooming summer?

Summer covers the months when most things are happening. There seems to be something in bloom all the time. There are literally thousands of plants from which to choose. Check carefully on the flowering times when you buy them so that you get an even spread in early mid and late summer. Do not forget to include some flowers for cutting for the house.

 ▶▶ Also see: Romantic planting p.26-7, Exotica p.54-5

Autumn colour

Acer
Amelanchier
Berberis
Betula
Carpinus betulus
Cornus
Cotinus
Cotoneaster
Crataegus
Euonymus
Liquidambar
Malus
Prunus
Rhus typhina
Sorbus
Stephandra

Winter flowering

Abeliophyllum distichum
Chimonanthus praecox
Cornus mas
Daphne mezereum
Eranthis hyemalis
Erica camea
Erica x darleyensis
Galanthus
Hamamelis
Helleborus
Iris ungicularis
Jasminum nudiflorum
Lonicera fragrantissima
L. x purpusii
L. standishii
Mahonia
Sarcococca
Viburnum x bodnantense
V. farreri
V. tinus

Autumn colour?

There are still a large number of plants in flower during the autumn, but the real essence of autumn is the changing colour of the foliage. In a small garden it is impossible to have a mass of autumnal trees but there is quite a number of small trees and bushes that give great pleasure at this time of year. Similar colour can be provided in the autumn by berries and fruit. These not only provide wonderful colour but also food for birds and small mammals throughout the autumn and winter

Winter-flowering plant?

Many gardeners are unaware of the range of flowering plants that are available during the winter months. Many are highly fragrant as they need to attract the few insects that there are around. Most make good cut flowers for inside.

Extending the season
Try and use shrubs and trees that have more than one season. Many will produce a blaze of colour from changing leaves in the autumn, as well as possibly a flush of colourful berries (above). At the other end of the year, bulbs, such as these snowdrops and crocuses (left) can be planted in gaps between other plants as they die back below ground soon after flowering.

the edible garden

There is nothing quite like vegetables and fruit fresh from the garden. Most garden vegetables are selected for flavour, whereas those sold in shops are bred for other qualities, such as being able to be transported without bruising, looking good, maturing at the same time for ease of harvest and so on; flavour comes low down on the list. However vegetable growing takes time and to provide all the family vegetables for a whole year requires a lot of space. That said, a surprising amount can be grown even in a small garden.

What is needed?
Most gardens will be able to grow vegetables. Most need a sunny situation and soil that is not sodden but reasonably moisture-retentive. The more fertile the soil the better so if possible add in as much well-rotted organic material (garden compost or farmyard manure) as possible.

Too big?
Some vegetables take up too much space and are best grown on an allotment or in a large garden. Rows of peas and beans take up a lot of space but can be grown up wigwams of canes or strings. Potatoes are space hungry, but fortunately they are cheap and so their space is better used for other vegetables. Rhubarb, asparagus and globe artichokes are all desirable but need a lot of space.

Winter supplies?
Often vegetables all mature at the same time and it is not possible to eat them all. Well, why not freeze what you cannot eat for use in the winter? Other vegetables such as onions, potatoes, carrots and other root crops can be stored in a garage or shed. The onions should be hung in skeins or nets while the root crops can be stored in just-moist sand.

Growing bags?
Quite a number of vegetables can be grown not in the open ground but in growing bags set on a patio against a wall. These bags contain compost plus specially formulated fertiliser suitable for growing such plants as tomatoes, peppers, aubergines, beans, lettuces and many others. It is essential that they are watered regularly, at least once a day in hot, dry weather.

Herb pots?
There is no reason why herbs should be grown in the ground. Save space and grow them in pots instead. As well as being productive these are also decorative. Many herbs, such as chives and sage can be grown in the flower beds as they are ornamental as well as useful.

Fruit?
Fruit can take up a lot of space, but if trees and shrubs are grown as cordons, fans or espaliers up against walls or fences then they using up unproductive space and are well worth the effort. It is necessary to net the plants as the fruit ripens or the birds will pinch the lot.

Delicious fruit
There is nothing quite like ripe fruit picked straight from the plant. Amongst the easiest to grow in a small garden is the strawberry. It can be grown in a small bed or in a container of some sort. Most people grow the lush large strawberry fruits, but why not grow a few of the small but delicious alpine strawberries?

 ▶ ▶ Also see: The nature garden p.42-3

Best value for space

beetroot
carrots
courgettes (zucchini)
dwarf beans
kohl rabi
leeks
lettuce
radishes
sprouting broccoli
tomatoes

Herbs worth growing

basil
bay
chives
marjoram
mint
parsley
rosemary
sage
tarragon

Home produce
There is no reason
why the small
gardener should
not grow a few
vegetables. Many
such as this cabbage
are decorative
as well as edible.
Various herbs are
other things that
can be grown to
great advantage
in a small garden,
either in a bed or
in a container.
Place it near the
kitchen door for
convenience.

nature garden

Looking after own own?

Natural areas in the garden give a home to wildflowers, while ponds not only provide drink and washing facilities for birds and small mammals, but are also home for dragonflies, and many other insects as well as frogs and newts. Trees and shrubs also provide essential food, shelter and nesting sites for birds.

Close to nature?

Apart from occasional excursions to the countryside, most people's closest contact with nature is in their garden. Many watch birds and mammals from the window or look at butterflies flitting between flowers in the summer. The gardener is in a unique position. Working with the soil, letting it run through the fingers, constantly looking at plants, in the bushes and under stones, the gardener is much more aware of the life that lives or passes through the garden. Even the weather comes under closer scrutiny than most people give it. To be a good gardener you have to learn to work with nature and not against it. That way the best results are obtained.

Education?

One big advantage of encouraging wildlife in the garden is that children can experience it at first hand and can be encouraged to respect and, indeed, not be frightened of it. The unknown is so often the cause of fear, and fluttering birds, flee-ridden hedgehogs, slimy slugs or hopping frogs, can all be terribly frightening if you are not familiar with them. Wild animals are not pets and should not be treated as such, but there is no harm in watching them and very occasionally handling them. It is extremely important to get to know the world in which we live.

Encouragement?

Encourage children to read about wildlife and keep records of all the animals and birds that they see. Once discovered, the pleasures of nature will stay with a child for life.

Conservation?

In the increasingly concrete world in which we live, any area of greenery is most welcome to the wildlife. Within minutes of filling a pond with water, for example, pond-loving insects are likely to appear. Even creating an ordinary garden will attract a large number of insects and birds, but by selecting the plants carefully, food and shelter can be supplied for a harsh winter that might otherwise not be available.

Protecting wildlife?

Conservation is not all about encouraging wildlife it is also about protecting it. Life is a very complex business with various aspects interacting in unforeseeable ways. Kill off one aspect of it, either deliberately or accidentally and the effects can snowball so that all kinds of animals and plants that seem to have no connection suddenly disappear. Whole scale use of chemicals caused such reactions and many gardeners have now turned against using them simply because they are not certain of the long term effect. Fortunately it is perfectly possible to garden without the use of chemicals, or at the least using only those that occur naturally.

Nature is forever

Don't run hot and cold over conservation and protection, for example don't put out food for the birds one day and not the next. Once they begin to rely on your hospitality it is essential to keep providing it. By all means keep pets, but do not encourage birds to feed on the lawn and then suddenly introduce a cat! If you do later decide to keep a cat as a pet, the best time to bring it to the house is late summer when less birds will be coming to feeding stations.

Helping hand
Creating a habitat in which nature thrives is not only satisfying but also increasingly important for the survival of both animals and plants. For example, as the number of farm ponds have declined with the demise of the working horse, so the garden pond has become one of the main breeding sites for frogs.

encouraging wildlife

Although there are very few places on earth where something living does not occur, there are some places more favoured than others. These are where the conditions are particularly suitable. Create suitable conditions where birds and animals will find food, shelter and nesting sites and they will adopt your garden. If it has been concreted over they will look elsewhere.

Wild food
One way of encouraging wild life to come to the garden as well as helping them to survive is to provide food and shelter. This can be done with bags of nuts, but it is better to plant shrubs and other plants that provide a natural source of food. Here a squirrel eats a nut fallen from a hazel bush, while below berberis berries await the birds' attention.

Berried plants
Berberis
Chaenomeles
Cotoneaster
Crataegus
Daphne
Euonymus europeus
Hippohaë rhamnoides
Ilex
Ligustrum
Malus
Rosa
Sorbus
Symphorocarpus
Viburnum opulus

Some bee and butterfly plants
Aster
Buddleja
Calamintha
Centranthus
Cephalaria
Coreopsis
Cotoneaster
Echinacea
Echinops
Erigeron
Eryngium
Escallonia
Hebe
Hedera
Helenium
Hesperis
Lavandula
Mentha
Nepeta
Salvia
Scabiosa
Sedum
Solidago
Thymus

Changing style?
Adopting a policy of encouraging wildlife is not at odds with wanting a beautiful garden, indeed the two often go together, the greater diversity of plants in the garden the better it will be from both points of view.

Food?
Food can be provided either by putting it out in the garden or by planting plants that will provide food in a more natural way. Bird-tables and hanging baskets of food are both simply ways of encouraging birds to the garden. However, planting bushes that will provide berries for autumnal and winter use will be a more natural source of food. Similarly, leaving on the dead stems of herbaceous plants will provide plenty of seeds and sheltering insects that birds will seek out.

 ▶ ▶ Also see: Ponds and streams p.50-1

Flower power?

Flowering plants also provide food for a number of insects that come to collect, pollen and nectar. Bees, butterflies and many other insects are attracted to the garden by particular plants and are beneficial to the garden. Old-fashion flowers, rather than modern cultivars are best for this as the latter often lack nectar.

Shelter?

As well as food, birds and other animals need shelter and nesting sites. Shrubs and trees provide these, particularly those with dense, tangled stems. In an area with small gardens, persuade a neighbour to plant a few shrubs, just over the fence from your own few shrubs, between you, you will create a much bigger haven. Even open trees that provide no opportunity for birds to build nests can be provided with nest boxes.

Water?

Ponds are a magnet for wildlife of all sorts. They not only provide drink for most types of animal but also a home for a great deal of insect and aquatic life. Colourful dragonflies are always most welcome. Fish are a bit more problematic as, unless the pond is a large one, they tend to eat most other aquatic life, usually while it is still at its egg or juvenile stage, thus negating the purpose of the pond. If you want fish, do not overstock your pond.

Sweet nectar
One of the greatest joys of the garden is to see that butterflies have adopted it as their home. They will only do this if there is a diversity of plants that produce nectar. Many of the old-fashioned or meadow flowers are best for this.

organic chemical-free gardening

Nature against nature
As well as making a delightful garden, a wide range of flowering plants also helps to attract ladybirds, hoverflies and other beneficial insects that prey on greenfly and other pests. In this way the gardener achieves a balance between good and bad insects and never has to spray against infestations of the latter.

Thankfully the days when gardeners spent most of their lives spraying chemicals over everything either to kill it or to make it grow are now virtually over. Sprays are still used but in a more responsible fashion, and on the whole they are safer. However, many gardeners now realise that it is not necessary to spray every time a bug or weed appears in the garden. Many slight problems or infestations can be lived with as they cause little or no damage. Problems are considerably reduced by using a mixture of flowering plants, especially old-fashioned ones that encourage hoverflies and lady birds, both of which prey on aphids.

What's in the soil?
There seems to be almost universal agreement now that well-rotted organic material is the best possible conditioner for soils. It not only provides nutrients but also improves the structure of the soil. While chemicals provide an instant fix as far as food is concerned, they do little for the soil.

Type of compost

	Advantages	Disadvantages
Farmyard manure	Excellent soil conditioner and nutrient provider	Not always easy to acquire, may contain weed seed
Leaf mould	Excellent soil conditioner and nutrient provider	Only usually available in small quantities
Garden compost	Make yourself so readily available, recycles materials	May contain weed seed if not properly made
Proprietary manures	Excellent soil conditioner and nutrient provider, convenient	Expensive
Seaweed	Excellent soil conditioner and nutrient provider	Only locally available, except in small quantities

Composts?
Compost all garden refuse except pernicious weeds, as well as any uncooked vegetable waste from the kitchen. Either make your own bins or buy a ready-made one. Similarly, compost any leaves that you can collect. However, do not raid your local woods or the woodland habitat will be destroyed.

Weeds?
The real secret is to keep on top of weeds and remove any that appear by hand. It is more difficult when clearing land for the first time. Smothering them with black polythene is one of the most popular methods if the soil is too heavy to remove them by hand while digging.

Slugs and snails?
Not all animals are welcome in the garden, slugs and snails being probably the least favoured. In the past the remedy has been to smother the garden with slug pellets, but these can be injurious to both pets and wildlife. The best way of reducing the problem to manageable proportions is to go out at night with a torch and round them up while they are feeding on your plants and move them to another site, preferably a long way from your garden. There are other traditional methods but this is the most effective.

Waste not
The addition of well-rotted organic material to the soil not only creates a better texture but also adds nutrients, thus reducing or eliminating the need to use chemical fertilisers. Compost bins can easily be constructed and can be used to recycle all organic waste from the garden and any uncooked vegetable waste, such as peelings, from the kitchen.

wild water

Water features

There is nothing quite like having water in the garden; it adds another dimension altogether. Even a small pool, perhaps one contained in a half-barrel, will provide a habitat for a few water plants as well as creating reflections from the surface that always draw the eye. Moving water, either in a stream or from a fountain or spout adds even more excitement. The tinkling or tumbling sound is very restful and helps to create a sense of peace and tranquillity in a garden, even if there is the roar of traffic in the background. The movement also creates a restless surface with reflections being thrown off in all directions.

Good, bad or indifferent?

Of all the features in a garden, those incorporating water are the most likely to be mishandled and to turn out to be an eyesore rather than a stunning attraction, often the idea is sound but the execution is takes a little extra planning. There is nothing worse than a half-empty pond with a few sad, marooned plants and a heavily creased liner showing above the water line. Think and plan carefully before you start. Take advice and use professional help if need be and the result will certainly be worth while.

Style?

There is the world of difference between a formal pond and a natural one. Decide when you are designing the garden, what are you trying to achieve, what style of water feature will best suit the overall design of the garden. In a small paved garden, a formal design will be better than trying to create a miniature natural pond. On the other hand in a larger garden, where the arrangement of plants is freer flowing then a natural pond may well be better suited. In many cases a semi-formal pond, one with hard edges but freely planted is likely to be the best choice. Unlike borders, ponds and other water features are difficult and expensive to change once they are installed, so plan carefully.

Moving water?

Moving water is a definite bonus in a garden and lucky is the gardener who has a natural stream running through the grounds. However, with ingenuity, it is possible to create a stream that looks natural, but again, nothing looks sadder than a badly constructed stream. The best streams are not those that take over the whole garden but those that are part of an overall design. A short one tumbling down waterfalls on a rock garden to a pool at the base can be very attractive and in keeping.

Plants?

A formal water feature, if of a strong enough design can stand on its own, but most need to have plants associated with them to look at their best. Even fountains and spouts can benefit from having at least some greenery around them, planted in pots if the surrounding area is paved. If there are fish in ponds or pools then it is essential that oxygenating plants are used. It is equally important that there are clear areas with no plants.

Maintenance?

Ponds and other water features do need to be maintained. Keep leaves and debris out of the water and every so often either empty the pond and clean it out or carefully dredge out the bottom. Great care must be taken if the pond has a liner as it is easy to puncture it. Do not allow plants to take over the pond or pool. Regularly remove any excess.

Tranquil water
A patch of water, no matter how small, and its surrounding plants add a touch of tranquillity to a garden. It also provides water for drinking and a habitat for many animals. Creating a small pool opens up a whole new range of beautiful plants that is denied to the gardener without water. Any extra work involved in creating and maintaining a pool is far outweighed by the pleasure it gives.

ponds and streams

Informal pools
Ponds that are fully integrated into the design of the garden work best. Above, the water cascades down into a rocky pool that merges into the lawn. Wooden decking (right) allows an intimate view of the water and its contents without looking at all intrusive. Small trees, and other plants soften the edges of both pools and helps them blend into the landscape.

Ponds and streams are fun to construct but they must be properly made if they are to be successful. Do not skimp on either time or materials.

Design underwater?
As well as the overall design of the pond in respect of the garden as a whole, the underwater profile of the pond should be considered. Aquatic plants like different depths of water and it is a good idea to create a series of ledges or steps round the pond so that planting baskets can be placed at the appropriate depth. A further consideration is to have a gradual slope at some point in the pond so that animals can easily reach the water's edge and birds have shallow water in which to bathe.

Installing flexible liners?
Dig a hole the for the final shape of the pond and line it with a soft sand. Lay the liner across the pond, held taut around its edges with bricks or stones. With a hosepipe pour water onto the liner, and as it fills it will gradually sink into the pond, taking up the excavated shape. Trim off the excess and bury the margins beneath the surrounding bank or under edging stones.

Planting ponds?
Apart from puddled clay ponds it is impossible to plant aquatic plants directly into the pond as there is no soil. The way to get round this is to use lattice pots, designed for ponds. Special pond potting compost should be used as ordinary compost is likely to float away, unless held in place by a layer of gravel.

 ▶▶ Also see: Encouraging wildlife p.44-5

Pond and Stream Liners

	Advantages	Disadvantages
Polythene	Cheap	Short life, difficult to install
PVC	Flexible, fit any shape of pool, easy to install	Superseded by LDPE, easily punctured
LDPE	Very flexible, fit any shape of pool, easy to install	Easily punctured
Butyl	Best flexible liner, easy to install, blends in well, relatively long life	Expensive, easily punctured
Rigid	Cheap, preformed	Fixed designs, limited sizes
Sectional	Rigid construction but in sections giving greater range of sizes	Still limitations in design
Concrete	Allows any shape to be made, long life	Can crack if not installed correctly, expensive
Puddled clay	Forms a natural pond, plants can be planted directly into it	Needs source of clay, must not dry out as it cracks

Formal pools
Above: In more formal situations, pools with clear-cut lines are preferable. Here the circular pond works well between the paved area and the cropped lawn. The formality has been toned down by the large amount of diverse foliage floating and growing in the water.

Streams?

Make streams look as natural as possible. They can emerge from one pool and descent to another or appear as a spring from under a rock to fall down to a pool. Pumps or vary capacities are available to lift the water, to create either a trickle or a torrent. Concrete makes a better liner than a flexible one unless the latter is really well disguised. Concrete soon takes on a natural, rocky appearance, especially if it has stones embedded in it.

Frozen ponds?

If you have fish it is not a good idea to let the pond freeze over as gases will build up and oxygen will become depleted. A pond heater will keep a small area free, alternatively stand a pan of hot water on the ice to create a hole. Do not break the ice as the shock waves may damage the fish. Concrete pools can be harmed by the pressure of ice. Rubber balls or lumps of polystyrene in the water will absorb the pressure.

fountains and spouts

Fountains and water spouts are ideal for small gardens, especially if there is no room for a pond, or if open water is considered dangerous because of young children. One of the great things about falling water, besides its sparkle and reflections, is the soothing tinkling sound that it makes. Although it may require a bit of time and effort to set up, the results are certainly worth it.

Fountains
Bubble fountains (above) not only making an interesting use of water, but are safe for children as there is no pool of water above ground. Traditional fountains (right) create a wonderful focal point in the garden as well as adding the delightful sound of tinkling water and sparkling patterns of reflected light.

Fountains?

A large range of different fountains are now available. They can be used as part of a pool or pond or they can be the sole purpose of the set up with the pool being part or the fountain. There are a large number of different spray patterns to choose from, some fountains offering several alternatives. It is also possible to get fountains that will automatically change their spray patterns every few seconds. Not all fountains need pools, the bubble fountains, where water bubbles out of a stone or the ground, is frequently set in a bed of large pebbles with the reservoir and pump hidden below. These are not only very attractive, especially in the small garden, but are also safe if there are young children around.

Wind?

When setting up a fountain, remember to take into account the strength of the wind. In a windy site a tall jet may be constantly blown away from the pool, so that the water falls outside. If strong winds are only of periodic nuisance then a tall jet can be switched off for the duration, but if they are frequent, choose a smaller jet.

 ▶ ▶ Also see: The Nature garden p.42-3

Spouts?

Spouts are single jets of water emitted from a pipe in a wall or column, falling into a basin, pool, or onto rocks or pebbles. There are many designs of spouts now available but some of the most popular are no more than a mask, of a lion for example, that is fixed to a wall in which there is concealed pipework descending to a pump and the pool. They are simple, relatively cheap, but very effective.

Pumps?

Pumps are now quite cheap and there is a wide range available. The more powerful the pump the bigger the possible jet. Most are submersible and are kept in the pond immediately below the fountain, but for bigger arrangements the pump is kept in pump chambers. Electricity and water is a dangerous mix, so get professional help if there is any doubt whatsoever about the installation of pumps or underwater lights.

Something different?

With modern electronics the old art of trick fountains can be carried further than was ever imaginable. These type of fountains are often made to come on suddenly, and can be startling. Using 'magic eyes' as switches, a row of fountains can be made to come on and off as a person walks along the path, or, a the fountain can spring into action as a visitor approaches it. With more expensive equipment they can even be made to dance to music or make complicated patterns. Lighting a fountain from below can create magical effects.

Spouting spouts

Water spouts have been used to create humourous situations in gardens for centuries. Not all need be as entertaining as this, but they can still be relied upon to create interest and to add another dimension to a garden that only water can provide.

exotica

Living on the wild side?

One advantage that a small garden, especially if it is enclosed, has over a larger one is that it can easily be transformed into an exotic oasis. This works particularly well on a small scale but is actually very difficult to carry off on a larger one. The extravagance of exotic plants creates a garden unlike any other type, dripping with foliage and mystery.

What is exotica?

Exotic plants, in a way, are classed as any plants that are nor native, but that is not quite enough because most plants that are grown in gardens come from other countries. Exotic plants on the whole tend to be big, flamboyant ones that often have their origins in the tropics or at least have the appearance of such. Large specimens of many of the plants may be quite expensive but many others can be very easily be grown from seed as annuals. Others are simply nothing more than basic house plants, available from any good florist or garden centre.

Exotic gardens?

These gardens are designed using a lot of this type of plant. The overall effect is almost that of a jungle with masses of foliage, much of it large leaved, with occasional splashes of vivid colours. Lit from below at night the garden has an eerie richness. It has not got the tranquillity of a romantic garden, but its grandeur is such that it transports the away from the everyday world into one in which they and their visitors can relax.

Many of the plants that can be used for this type of garden are tender and will not stand the winter's extreme frosts. However, they are perfectly happy outside during the summer and they can either be grown as annuals or grown in containers and moved inside during the colder months.

Inside or out?

This kind of garden can be created either inside or out. A hot steamy conservatory can house exotic plants throughout the year, with no change in the seasons, just as in the tropics but unlike that of the native country. One of the best ideas is to link the house and the garden. The conservatory or glass house is used during the winter months and then the doors are thrown open and the inside merges with the outside as the exuberant growth continues in the garden. This is by far one of the best types of design for fully integrating the house and the garden.

Winter days?

With the use of conservatories or garden rooms, the illusion of eating and relaxing outside can be carried out throughout the year including the winter. Cane or cast iron furniture, frequently painted white, is the traditional furnishings amongst the rich foliage. It is also a good idea to consider including water elements such as pools and fountains to add to the general atmosphere.

Can these gardens be anywhere?

Outside gardens are best where the temperature is at least relatively mild and there is reasonable rainfall. In cold areas they are really only going to be a summer garden, but then it is unlikely that much time would be spent outside any during harsh winters. There is no reason why an exotic garden cannot be kept anywhere under glass as long as it is possible to heat it.

Grass roots
Exotica exists in many forms. It can be brash and colourful or it can be simply different and unusual. Grasses are common enough, but used in this way against a background of bamboo they create a wild, lush image that is very exotic in its appeal.

under glass

Visual links
A conservatory, bursting with life and energy, becomes part of the scene beyond. This tropical area not only creates a wonderful area for sitting and relaxing, but visually links the inside of the house with the planted garden beyond.

Many gardeners see the greenhouse as a means to an end; simply a place to propagate plants for the garden, or to raise tomatoes and cucumbers. However others see them in a completely different light, for them they are place to keep exotic plants of one sort or another. Some simply like to grow various plants and vegetables and keep them in serried ranks on shelves, others create more of an indoor garden. With conservatories much more generally available the possibilities of creating a stunning indoor garden are increased, particularly an indoor garden that can be enjoyed throughout the year.

Temperatures?

It is important to decide whether the conservatory is simply for plants or also for living in, as much will depend on this. For living and entertaining, the temperature should not be too high and the humidity should be low. Tropical plants on the other hand need higher temperatures and high humidity to do well. There are plenty of plants that do not have these requirements and an effective garden room can still be created. However if the heart is set on growing tropical plants then it may be possible to divide the conservatory in two keeping one part hotter than the other. Alternatively it is always possible to install a greenhouse within the conservatory!

Heating?

If the exotic garden is created within a conservatory then it may be possible to extend the house's central heating into it. If not independent heaters will be required. These can be simple electric heaters or a hot water or air system can be run from a small boiler. The air may be too dry for many plants and so it might be necessary to include a humidifier in the system. Alternatively pools with waterfalls or fountains will help to keep the air buoyant.

Greenhouses?

It is easier to grow exotic plants in a greenhouse as it does not usually serve the dual function of the need to house people as well as plants. The temperature and humidity can therefore be maintained to serve the plants rather than people. There is also not the necessity to create a garden as such, the plants can be arranged more for convenience than for show. However it is just as easy to turn a greenhouse into a feature as it is a conservatory and once climbers begin to hang from the roof it quickly becomes a rather interesting place. Having said that there is nothing wrong with using a greenhouse in a more conventional manner, for growing pot plants to take in the house when they are in flower, for propagating plants and for growing crops such as tomatoes or grapes.

Maintenance?

Watering and feeding are the keys to success. Being under heated glass the compost in which the plants are growing can dry out very quickly. Automatic watering systems, including standing plants on capillary matting will make life considerably easier. Because of the amount of watering required, nutrients get leached from the compost very quickly and thus the

plants will need feeding at least once a week during the period when they are in growth. Shade is something else to take seriously. Most tropical plants are shielded from the sun be the tall forest above them and blinds will be needed for both greenhouses and conservatories if the plants are to be happy. The third requirement is ventilation. Even though the houses must be kept warm, it is also important that the receive adequate ventilation or the stagnant air will promote diseases. The warm moist conditions are ideal for both diseases and pests. One way to avoid them is by scrupulous hygiene. Remove any rotting vegetation or dead leaves as soon as you see them. Tackle any outbreaks of pests or diseases as soon as you notice them, before they can get hold.

Controlled exotica

A more controlled exotic interior. Here the plants are grouped in containers, creating islands of greenery, the overall effect being of lush cool foliage, although the temperature can become quite high.

exotic plants

Exotic plants should remind one of tropical gardens, but they may be plants that happily grow in far more temperate climates. Bamboos for example, have a certain exotic appeal but many are perfectly hardy, as are ferns. While it is possible to use tropical climbers inside, it is often difficult to use them in the open garden.

Orchids rule
Orchids are among the most popular flowers of all time. Although there are many hardy species, it is the more tropical varieties, such as this *Phalaeuapsis* hybrid, that most people would like to grow in their conservatory.

Keypoints

Watering
Feeding
Heating
Shading
Ventilation
Hygiene

Houseplants?

Many houseplants make perfect specimens for use in an exotic garden, both inside and out. During the summer move some of the house plants outside, they will not only enjoy the conditions but will also provide an exotic touch to the patio. Aspidistras, coleus, spider plants and many others can all be moved as long as the night time temperature does not fall too low, say not below about 15°C (59°F).

Climbers and trailers?

Plants that climb and trail are important to the overall effect. Hot house plants such as glory lily (Gloriosa) and Monstera deliciosa, can be used in heated conservatories, but outside substitutes must be used. Simple ivy, Hedera is extremely effective and is also tough enough to withstand battering winds. Passion flowers, Passiflora, have very exotic flowers and fruit and are hardy, particularly if grown against a wall. For real colour in the conservatory how about bougainvillea?

Orchids?

The one plant that nearly everybody would like to grow is the orchid. While there are a few that can be grown outside, these are not particularly exotic, it is the tropical ones that capture people's imagination and these must be grown inside. Growing orchids can become obsessive and rather expensive, so think carefully before letting them take over your lives. On the other hand you could end up with a hobby for life.

Foliage?

Ferns, hostas, bamboos and phormiums are all hardy plants that can be used, although there are tender examples of them all that can be grown inside. *Fatsia japonica*, various rubber plants (Ficus) and bananas (Musa) are shrubby examples. Many flowering plants have excellent foliage, camellias and cannas for example. Some can be grown regularly from seed. The castor oil plant, Ricinus, being a good example of one with excellent foliage.

 ▶ ▶ Also see: Romantic planting p 26-7

Flower power?

Orchids have already been mention, but there are plenty of other plants besides these. Datura or brugmansia as some of them are now known, are magnificent plants with a heady scent. Strelitzia has a very exotic look, but so then do lots of relatively common plants like busy lizzies, Impatiens.

Maintenance?

Watering and feeding are the keys to success. Being under heated glass the compost in which the plants are growing can dry out very quickly. Automatic watering systems, including standing plants on capillary matting will make life considerably easier. Because of the amount of watering required, nutrients get leached from the compost very quickly and thus the plants will need feeding at least once a week during the period when they are in growth. The warm moist conditions are ideal for both diseases and pests. One way to avoid them is by scrupulous hygiene. Remove any rotting vegetation or dead leaves as soon as you see them. Tackle any outbreaks of pests or diseases as soon as you notice them, before they can get hold.

Desert days

Above: Desert plants of various types add a different exotic dimension to many gardens and conservatories. They have the advantage of not needing much attention, needing far less watering and feeding than the more lush tropical exotica.

Hardy and tender

Left: An exotic garden is created from a mixture of hardy and tender plants. The bright brash colours are set off well against the luxuriant foliage, giving a tropical feeling to the scene. Foliage plays a very important part in exotic gardens and attention should be given to choosing plants with interesting shapes, colour and texture.

quick tricks

Bigger is better?

There can be few gardeners who are content with the size of their garden, most feel they want something larger. However, it is possible with a bit of design trickery to make the garden look much bigger than it really is. Even a small basement garden can appear to be doubled in size with a little bit of effort.

There are other tricks that help to draw the eye where the gardener wants it to go, towards something attractive or away from something ugly perhaps. It is also possible to help make an immature garden appear as if it has been there for some time.

Instant gardens?

When moving into a new house, many people want their gardens to look good as quickly as possible; they want an instant garden. In truth it takes a while to establish a garden, but if you are prepared to go out and buy mature plants then it is possible to fill up a garden very quickly. However it is often a good idea to live with a garden for a while before finally deciding what you want to do with it. In the meantime why not use plants in pots? A magnificent display can be created using these as a temporary planting. The plants can be bright annuals or they can be perennials or shrubs. Both the perennials and shrubs can be used later when the garden has been established.

Annuals?

Another way of getting a splash of colour is to fill any existing borders with annuals, either using plants, or more cheaply just scattering packets of seed. If there are no borders then dig some temporary ones.

Instant cover?

Laying paving and other solid surfaces takes time and can be quite expensive. However it is possible to lay surfaces either for paths or a terrace in a comparatively short time if it comes from a bag. Gravel is a magnificent boon to the instant gardener. First prepare the surface, tamp it down and then pour the gravel over it. It creates a very attractive surface right from the start and can be used as soon as it is laid. To start with the gravel will get pushed down into the soil and some areas will wear thin, but the odd bag tipped over it will refresh it in a matter of seconds. Another option would be to create a softer surface with chipped bark in similar speed.

Instant lawns?

Sown lawns take a while to become mature enough for any activity to take place on them. However, lawns laid from turfs come into use much more quickly. However, don't be tempted to skimp on the preparation, it is important to make certain that the site is level and that all perennial weeds have been removed or they will only regrow and become hopelessly mixed into the lawn.

Marking time?

Once you start to establish a garden to the finished design, it will naturally take a while to mature and grow to fill the space. It is a good idea to fill in the gaps with annuals or temporary planting so that the immature shrubs and perennials do not look lost in a sea of soil. As well as creating a visual effect, the annuals will also act as a ground cover and help keep the growth of weeds to a minimum.

Seeing is believing
A small garden can be extended way beyond its boundaries with the aid of the paint brush. This town garden looks out onto a mythical countryside that only exists in the eye of the beholder. The use of *trompe-l'oeil* is a skilled art but one that can really enhance a garden.

creating focal points

Focal points are essential components of garden design. Consider positioning a particular plant or garden object in such a way as to catch the eye.

Drawing the eye?
There are several reasons for drawing the eye in a garden. One is simply to draw attention to a particularly attractive feature. If the focal point is at the end of a path or lawn, then it helps to give the impression that the garden is bigger than it is, as it draws the eye down past everything else. On the other hand, a focal point in a border tends to break the monotony and add interest. One very useful application is to draw the eye away from something else. A container of bright flowers will make the viewer ignore an adjacent border that has finished flowering, or a fountain will keep the eye from wandering off to a neighbour's ugly garage that shows above the hedge.

Structures?
Summer houses, gazebos, make good focal points, people are always attracted to them even if they do not linger there for long. The higher quality the design the better as they are a prominent feature if they are used as a focal point. Place at the end of a broad path or on an edge of the lawn, hidden in the trees or shrubs that make quite a different point and with skill a cheaper one can be used.

Furniture?
Even a humble bench can be a draw in a garden. A white wooden or iron seat at the end of a curve in a path will pull the eye. Once seated the eye looks back along the vista and this can make a restful place to sit.

Far away
This small garden is made to look much larger by the constriction of the bordered pathway taking the eye down to a lawn that expands to an unseen size, way beyond sight. It is further increased by the eye being dawn into the apparent distance to the focal point of the fountain glistening and tinkling away. This is a good example of simple visual effects increasing the size of the garden.

Sculpture?
Off-the peg reproduction sculpture is widely available and relatively cheap. Original sculpture is far more expensive but usually much more interesting and satisfying. Again good positions are generally at the end of paths or lawns, but they also work very well partly submerged in foliage, particularly amongst shrubs.

Containers?
Large containers such as urns, can be used instead of sculpture, especially if they are stood on plinths and are very effective at drawing the eye, particularly again at the end of or at a bend in a path. Smaller containers of plants can be stood in borders where flowers are beginning to flag to perk them up and to create something of interest for the eye.

Flower power?
The cheapest method of creating a focal point is with a plant. It has to be a plant that is decidedly different from its neighbours or it will disappear into the background. A bright yellow lily growing amongst the green foliage of a shrubbery, or a blue delphinium amongst a border of yellow flowers will always stand out. On the other hand, specimen plants standing by themselves will also draw the eye. A pampas grass at the ends of the lawn, perhaps where it catches the evening sun, can be very effective, as can a solitary columnar conifer.

 ▶ ▶ Also see: Container planting p.12-3, Year-round interest p.36-7

Full stops
Remove the urn at the end of this pergola and the result would be a dead end of no particular significance. Leave the urn where it is and the eye immediately travels towards it, creating a full stop and at the same time enhancing the visual quality of the elegant walkway although it is in no way physically connected to it.

garden deceits

What the eye does not see

By nature man is a curious animal. Curve a pathway out of sight and he will want to know what lies round the corner. His mind always seems to imagine that there is something more interesting just out of sight. This is a useful device for increasing the apparent size of a garden: a pathway that disappears must lead to another part of the garden, even if in reality it come to a blank wall.

There are various tricks that can be used in gardens to make them appear to be something they are not. Size is usually the main area of deceit with gardeners wanting to make their gardens appear bigger, location or setting is another. Once you begin to think creatively, the possibilities are endless.

Mirage?

In very small gardens, such as small basement areas, the size can appear to be doubled by the careful use of one or more mirrors. Unless studying it carefully (or trying to walk through it) anyone looking at the mirror will think they see more garden beyond a doorway or window, when it is in fact the reflection of the garden they are in.

Trompe-l'oeil?

Another trick is to create a *trompe-l'oeil*, 'trick of the eye'. In its simplest form this is just a painting on a wall or fence that is so life-like that it looks real. A painting of a doorway with

more garden beyond looks just that, and deceives the eye into thinking the garden is much bigger than it really is. A painting with countryside and animals, cows or sheep perhaps, transforms a town garden to a rural one. Sometimes the *trompe-l'oeil* can be three dimensional. A popular trick is fix trellis to a wall that has a distorted perspective and appears to recede into the distance. Inside the trellis arch there may be a painting or even a mirror to depict what lies through the gap, or even a view through to a neighbour's garden, which is not trickery but cheating!

▶ ▶ Also see: Disguising essentials p.122-3

A bigger lawn?

Mowing the lawn in stripes that go away from the viewer will make the lawn look much longer. Have the lines go across the grass and the lawn will seem shorter.

Longer paths?

A similar effect can be obtained with brick paths by laying the bricks lengthways along the path, this draws the eye ever onwards, giving the impression that it is much longer than it is. Place the bricks across the path and the eye is stopped as if by a barrier and the path seems shorter.

Colour assisted?

The use of pale colours, especially misty blues at the end of a border will make the border look further away than it is (in the same ways as hills look further away on a misty day than on a bright one). On the other hand bright reds will seem to be closer than their true position.

Disappearing into the unknown?

Another trick to consider when laying out the garden, is to ensure that it is not possible to see the whole thing in one glance. Design it in such a way that paths curve away behind shrubs or trellises to create the impression that the garden goes on and on out of sight. Skillfully handled it should be possible to have somebody walk round in a circle, round the whole garden, thinking that they still have not got to the bottom of it yet.

Shining example

Mirrors are excellent devices for increasing the size of a garden; they are unexpected and so easily fool people into misinterpreting what they see. This one, placed at the end of a small pool, reflects the garden in such a way that it seems to carry on beyond the boundary. Softening the edges of the mirror with trellising and climbers helps to disguise what it truly is.

arches and trellises

A flat, two-dimensional garden is generally rather boring. Once it is lifted into the third dimension with shrubs and small trees it starts to become far more interesting. However, these take time to grow and mature. An instant way of gaining height is to erect trellising. This has several important functions. In the first instance it is a support for climbers, a very important group of plants. These not only increase the height of the garden, by taking the plants upwards, but also act as screens. Arches provide the means from moving from one area to the next through these screens and are a very important part of any garden.

Framing the beyond

As well as physically supporting gates, arches have a very important visual role to play. They frame a section of what lies beyond and thus entices the viewer to enter. The framing can be a simple arch such as brick or hedging, but structure becomes very attractive if used to support climbing plants, such as roses seen here.

Internal screens?

Plant screens are useful for preventing the eye from seeing all of the garden at once, but at the same time provide tantalising glimpses of what lies beyond. The next part of the garden is only revealed once you pass through a gap or arch. Breaking a garden, even a small one, down into several compartments or individual gardens, makes it far more interesting and also makes it seem larger. Internal screens not only deflect the eye but also the wind. In breezy areas, the more hedges and trellises there are, the less damage the wind is going to cause.

Boundary screens?

Boundary screens also help greatly with the problem of reducing wind damage. They also give privacy both from prying eyes and also noise. It is quicker to grow plants over trellising than it is to grow a hedge and is also more colourful.

Arches?

Arches are wonderful things for the garden. They are the means that one moves from area to another. When approaching, the next area of the garden can be glimpsed but not all is revealed until one passes through. They also act as supports for climbing plants, so that the passage from one are to the next is a pleasant one, especially so if the flowers are fragrant. There are many different designs, from formal to rustic and they can be purchased ready made or home made.

Plants for arches and trellises
Clematis
Cobaea scandens
Humulus
Ipomoea
Lathyrus odoratus
Lonicera
Rosa
Solanum crispum
Solanum jasminoides
Thunbergia alata
Vitis

 ▶ ▶ Also see: Entrances and exits p.88-9, Inner boundaries p.120-1

Pergolas and walkways?

Pergolas are a series of arches connected together to form a walkway. It can be purely a structure but it looks much better if it is covered with climbers. A path disappearing through a pergola tends to make the garden look much bigger and can be a very pleasant way of joining one area to another. Fragrant climbers, such as wisteria, honeysuckle or roses are especially good. However, if the pergola is relatively narrow, avoid prickly roses.

Materials and design?

Trellises can be made of plastic or wood. Plastic is really only suitable for very small areas and preferably attached to walls or solid fences. Wood is far more sympathetic to the garden as well as being much stronger. There is a very wide range of designs, both in the way the wood over-laps but also in the overall shape of the trellis. The supporting posts usually benefit by some form of finial on their tops. Arches can also be made from wood, but proprietary ones are also made from metal or plastic, the latter may not last for very long. Arches can also be made by extending an adjacent hedge. A more formal arch can be constructed from bricks.

Cool walkways
Pergolas are a series of connected arches, usually covered with climbers and placed along a path or walkway. As well as creating an enticing tunnel of flowers, often fragrant, they make a beautiful shaded walkway or even sitting area. Roses, clematis or plants with large tassels of flowers such as laburnum or wisteria, seen here, are all good candidates for clothing the structure.

flower power

Flower people?

To many people the whole purpose of a garden is to have flowering plants; not all would agree as they do take up a bit more time than, say, just growing shrubs. However, the extra time is well worth it and it need not be excessive anyway. Annuals and bedding plants, for example, once planted take up little time and yet go on flowering cheerfully well into autumn. On the other hand, perennials tend to have a more restricted flowering period but this gives the opportunity to have a border or garden that constantly changes in appearance, as some plants fade and others come into flower.

Flowers in the garden?

How does one fit flowers into the design of a general garden? The conventional way is to create a series of borders around a central lawn. This can be attractive but for many it may boring. A good alternative is a sinuous path meandering between two borders filled with flowering plants creating a very pleasant place to wander; one feels more in contact with the flowers than if looking at them from the middle of a lawn. If the garden is very small, flowering plants can be displayed in containers. These can be stood on a patio or they can be used in a more three-dimensional display on the side of steps, or by using hanging baskets or window boxes.

Flowers for colour?

Choose the combination of flower colours as carefully as you would for clothing or room furnishings. The colours should blend together harmoniously, perhaps with the odd bit of discord to enliven things. Softer colours are more restful and easier to combine, strong colours add a touch of excitement to a garden, especially hot reds and oranges but like parties, too many can be too much of a good thing and will soon become boring. Try to blend colours, moving gently from one to another, avoid dotting different colours all over the place so that the result is spotty. The eye finds it difficult to find somewhere to rest in a spotty border, whereas merging patches of colour are more harmonious and pleasant to the eye.

Flowers for fragrance?

There is a tendency to think of flowers just in terms of colour but there is often much more to them than that. Fragrance is also a quality that endears many of them to gardeners. In a small garden every flower should be made to pay its way and if there is a choice between a flower of a certain colour and another flower of the same colour but with a perfume, go for the perfumed one every time. There are so many flowers to choose from that the small gardener should be able to choose a fragrant one nearly every time.

Flowers for cutting?

One of the nicest things about growing plants in the garden is that there is always something that can be cut and taken indoors. If possible devote a small corner for growing special flowers just for cutting. It can be part of the vegetable garden or even in the greenhouse. Many plants can be included in a border. Chrysanthemums and dahlias, for example, are excellent cut flowers and can either be grown in a special area or as part of the colourful scene in a border.

Dried flowers?

Some flowers dry better than others and if a winter arrangement is required it is worth growing a few plants with this in mind. Potpourri is also a wonderful reminder of summers past and flowers suitable for inclusion may also be considered.

Painting with flowers
While foliage gives a garden structure and permanence, flowers add the glitter and provide an ever-changing scene. No two days are the same, as more flowers come into bloom, others fade away. As the different varieties come into flower, so the colours change along with shapes and textures. The combinations are infinite and since they are not permanent, the gardener is free to experiment.

bedding plants

For that instant colourful garden, there is nothing quite like annuals and bedding plants. They are cheap, cheerful and readily available. They can be used in the border, in pots, hanging baskets or window boxes and they last throughout the summer and into autumn.

Annuals and bedding plants

Annuals, which also include a number of tender perennials such as pelargoniums, are extremely useful plants in the garden. They come rapidly into flower and last for a very long time, making these ideal for the instant gardener or for the busy gardener. On the whole they are bright colours and are therefore more suited to a brash colour scheme, but they are always guaranteed to brighten up the scene.

Growing from seed?

The cheapest way of buying annuals is to buy the seed and grow them yourself. Most packets contain plenty of seed and so quite a number of plants can be grown for a small outlay. Most annuals prefer to be germinated in a warm environment, which means a propagator, but in small quantities they can be grown indoors in a light (but away from direct sun), warm position. Some annuals are hardy and can be sown where they are to grow either in the previous autumn or in the spring. Tender annuals should only be sown outside once the threat of frosts is past.

Buying?

To save the trouble of growing annuals from seed, they can be purchased as seedlings or small plants from a nursery or garden centre. There is not such a wide selection available as there is from seed, but there is still a fair range to chose from. Be careful not to plant out tender annuals before all frosts have gone or you are likely to have to start again.

Containers?

Annuals make superb containers. There is an ever increasing range of trailing plants that are suitable for hanging baskets and window boxes as well as sturdier ones for larger containers on the patio and elsewhere. Their one drawback is that they need constant watering, usually once a day, and even more frequently in hot, dry weather.

 ▶ ▶ Also see: Fascinating foliage p.77, Romantic planting

Bedding?

Bedding schemes have gone a little out of fashion in recent times, but they still have a lot going for them if you like brash colours and a fairly instant garden. One big advantage is that you can have a completely different garden each year, simply by changing the colours and the planting plan. Different colours are best used as blocks rather than random planting.

Mixed borders?

There is a lot to be said for mixing the different types of plants so that you get the best of all worlds. Create a herbaceous and shrub, border which provides the form and structure and fill the gaps with annuals for bright and continuous colour.

Colourful annuals

Ageratum
Alonsoa
Antirrhinum
Argyranthemum
Begonia semperflorens
Bidens ferulifolia
Brachycome iberidifolia
Borago officinalis
Centaurea cyanus
Cerinthe major
Clarkia
Collinsia bicolor
Cynoglossum
Echium
Helichrysum
Iberis
Impatiens
Lobelia erinus
Lobularia maritima
Nigella damascena
Osteospermum
Pelargonium
Petunia
Phacelia
Rudbeckia
Salvia hormium
Scabiosa
Senecio cinerea
Tropaeolum
Verbena x hybrida
Viola x wittrockiana

Versatility

A handful of different plants can provide a multitude of colour choices and can be used in all kind of different situations. Frequent watering and deadheading is all that is required to keep them fresh for a long period. Seen here are *Petunia* 'Million Bells Blue' (left) *Begonia Rheimantha* 'Love Me' (above top) and impatiens (above) in a container.

herbaceous plants

Herbaceous plants are perennials and come up every year. They usually take a year or so to reach their final size and so a border containing them is not so instant as one containing solely annuals. Although there are many brightly-coloured perennials, on the whole their colours are more subtle than annuals and allow more variety when designing a border. Generally, perennials are bulkier, more substantial plants and give the border a more solid, three-dimensional appearance. Most do not flower for such a long period as annuals, but this can be an advantage rather than a disadvantage as it means that the border can be a changing scene, whereas it is possible to get a bit bored with the same annuals all summer and autumn.

Borders?

It is borders where perennials excel. Few small gardeners can hope to have enormous herbaceous borders disappearing into the distance, but a surprisingly large number of interesting plants can be packed into a small garden. On the other hand a good display can be put on by relatively few plants. Most are easy to propagate, especially by division and large stocks can be built up very cheaply to allow them to be planted in quantity so that drifts of colour are produced.

Colours and shapes

One of the important things about herbaceous perennials is their sheer variety. They not only come in an infinite range of colours, but also sizes, shapes and textures. As well as solid blocks of colour, here there are furry plumes and airy clouds, accented with bright spots of colour. There are plants for all soils and positions. It is very difficult to imagine gardening without them.

Individual specimen plants?

Herbaceous plants are generally thought of as being primary plants for the border but they have many other uses. Many make excellent specimen plants, either to be used in isolation or to stand out in a border as a focal point. Pampas grass, for example makes an excellent plant for a central feature on a lawn. Others do well filling an odd corner by themselves in an eye-catching way. Euphorbia characias wulfenii, for example, makes a superb green mound with its yellow-flower-like bracts drawing attention to it for a long part of the year.

Mixed plantings?

Perennials mix very well with shrubs and trees and for the modern small garden this is probably the best combination. The trees and shrubs provide the structure and a green environment, while the herbaceous plants produce the colour mixed into it. The shrubs ensure that there is something of interest all year, even in the winter.

Containers?

Although annuals and tender perennials dominate the container scene, perennials are also often used. They look particularly good when they used on their own. For example a large container of acanthus can look astounding as can one containing a collection of blue or white agapanthus.

Easy perennials for cutting

Achillea	Gypsophila
Alstroemeria	Heliopsis
Aster	Liatris
Chrysanthemum	Physalis
Convallaria majalis	Rudbeckia
Dianthus	Solidago
Eryngium	

 ▶▶ Also see: Perennials for foliage p.78-9, Seasonal plants and shrubs p.38-9

Treatment?

Perennials are not difficult plants to grow as long as the ground is well prepared before they are planted. Some may need staking to prevent them flopping over in wind or rain, but this can be avoided, leaving cutting them down in the autumn as the only main activity – Some plants are more thirsty than others but it is possible to choose plants that will tolerate a

certain amount of drought and so the necessity to water is minimised. Indeed if plenty of organic material has been added to the soil and the border mulched, there should be no need to water at all. Most perennials benefit from being dug up and divided every four years. Throw away the woody centre part of the plants and replant the outer young sections.

Dreamy drifts
One of the best ways of using herbaceous material is to plant them in blocks or groups so that they form drifts of colour, merging into each another.

alpine and rock plants

Serious alpine gardeners grow a wide range of plants, many of which are ungrowable by those that do not have the required skills. They grow plants from the high mountain ranges that need very special conditions and which will not tolerate the hurly-burly of an ordinary garden border. On the other hand there are gardeners who simply like the effect that a rock garden gives to a garden and are content to grow easy but attractive plants in it, such as aubrieta. In-between the two are numerous plants that are little known to general gardeners but are attractive and are not too difficult to grow. Growing alpine plants can become addictive and with the possible exception of roses, there are more gardeners specialising in alpines than any other area.

Common or garden
Rock gardens and other rocky structures need not be devoted to high alpine plants that are difficult to grow. There are plenty of quite common plants, such as this aubrieta, that are easy to grow and put on a delightful colourful display.

Rock gardens?
Rock gardens are the main outward sign of growing alpines. It is not simply a heap of earth with a few stones dotted on it, but should be properly constructed with a free-draining mixture of loam and grit and rocks that are laid to represent the strata of an outcrop with at least a third of the rock buried beneath the soil to provide stability and cool root-runs for the plants. Plants are planted on the ledges and in the vertical crevices between the rocks. Any bare soil mixture is usually covered with a topdressing of gravel or small stones.

Raised beds?
Many alpine gardeners are not so interested in the overall effect of their plants, but are more concerned with creating the right conditions in which each plant may grow. While rock gardens may look pretty, they can get the same conditions by creating a raised bed with a brick or block surround filled with the same free-draining mixture. It is easier to tend and if designed well can still look very attractive.

Troughs?
On a smaller scale many plants are grown in square containers, originally old animal feeding and drinking troughs made from stone, but are now likely to be an old sink or a home made replica. These are suitable for growing really small alpine plants and for creating miniature landscapes using small pieces of stone for rocks. Again a very free-draining mixture of good loam and grit is required with some leafmould to hold sufficient moisture for the plant's needs.

Easy rock-garden plants

Aethionema	Globularia
Anthirrhinum (small species)	Leontopodium
Aquilegia (small species)	Linaria alpina
Armeria	Lewisia
Aubrieta	Origanum (small species)
Aurinia (syn. Alyssum)	Oxalis
Campanula (small species)	Papaver (small species)
Daphne	Phlox subulata
Dianthus	Primula
Draba	Saxifraga
Dryas octopetala	Sedum (small species)
Erinus alpinus	Sempervivum
Erodium	Silene acaulis
Gentiana	Thymus

▶ ▶ Also see: Fountains and spouts p.52-3

Alpine houses?

Most alpines are thoroughly hardy but many are susceptible to damp, mild winters and therefore need some protection, as much from the rain as from the cold. Alpine houses are basically the same as greenhouses except that they have much more ventilation. Even in the winter the windows are left open for air to circulate, except when rain or snow is likely to blow in. The staging is usually very strongly constructed as each contains a deep layer of sand into which the pots are sunk. This helps keep the roots warm in winter and cool in summer as well as keeping the compost just damp with moisture creeping in from the sand through the holes in the base of the pot or through the sides in the case of terracotta pots. Here some of the most difficult and precious plants are grown.

Alpine glories
The piercing blue of *Gentiana verna* (above) and the delicate poppies *Papaver alpinum* (left) are two of the many rewards of rock gardening. Growing specialist plants can be difficult but can become addictive. It is an ideal form of gardening for the keen gardener short of space but prepared to spend time tending plants.

fascinating foliage

Why foliage?

Many gardens are designed entirely for continuous flowering, but this can become rather overpowering. A well balanced garden also depends on foliage for its appearance. Foliage not only acts as a foil or a background for flowering plants, but is also attractive in its own right.

Shades of green?

Although most plants have green leaves, the number of different shades of green seem to be infinite. Many gardeners get pleasure from this alone. However there is a very wide range of colours in foliage from almost white, through cream and yellow to gold, and from blue to dusky purple.

Mixed colours?

Some of the more interesting leaves are a mixture of two or more colours. Most frequently they are green and yellow or cream, but there are also many other subtle variations. Variegated foliage is fascinating but it should be used with care. Too much in one place becomes rather messy and unpleasant to look at. It is much better to have one or two well-chosen plants mixed in with normal green foliage. In this way the variegated foliage creates a bigger impact and is much more appreciated than if there is a whole swathe of it.

Texture?

The texture of the leaves is important. Some, such as camellias, are shiny. These glint in the light and are useful for placing in a dark spot or between dull-leaved shrubs. On the other hand there are those covered with hairs giving a velvety look. Those of lambs ears (Stachys byzantina) are very furry as their name suggests, giving the plant a rich silver texture.

Shape?

Individual leaves present a great range of shape and size. Big gunnera leaves are like giant rhubarb leaves and have a very dramatic impact, especially in a small garden. Irises and the like produce spiky leaves which make an interesting contrast to, say, the filigree of ferns, or to the more solid foliage of hostas.

Prickles?

The shape of some leaves are enhanced by prickles. Holly, for example, has very interestingly shaped leaves with the margins, rising up into sharp needles. The prickles have been developed by the plant to prevent browsing by animals and can still be put to good effect. Holly makes an impenetrable hedge, for example, or a wonderful deterrent when grown up a wall.

Foliage only?

It is possible to have a garden that consists of entirely foliage. With skill, utilising different colours, shapes and textures, this could be a very interesting garden, and one that would take little looking after. The most extreme example of this is a garden covered entirely in ivy, which is allowed to ramp over everything including hummocks of earth and objects such as tree stumps, giving a three-dimensional effect.

Foliage for cutting?

Foliage is also an important element in flower arranging, especially during the winter when there are few flowers around. When considering which foliage plants to grow this is always worth bearing in mind.

Beautiful foliage
Foliage is often overlooked in a garden where colourful flowers dominate. However, it is worth considering carefully as it can introduce a lot of interest to a garden. It is often fascinating in its own right, such as this canna, as well as providing a background against which the flowers stand out. Foliage often has the advantage that it lasts longer than the flowers and therefore adds a sense of continuity to the ever-changing borders.

perennials for foliage

Green filigree
It would be difficult to imagine a garden without ferns. They are amongst the most handsome of foliage plants and many have the advantage of being able to grow in shady conditions. Many have divided foliage, one of the most delicate being this *Adiantum venustum*. Those with shiny leaves are excellent for brightening up dull spots.

Although mainly thought of as flowering plants, perennials make excellent foliage plants. Many are grown simply for their foliage. Hostas, for example, are grown mainly for the decorative effect of their leaves, although, of course, they also produce flowers. While some plants are specifically grown for their foliage, there are many others that have a dual purpose. Montbretia (*Crocosmia*) which is mainly grown for its orange or yellow flowers also has very elegant strap-like leaves, which give interest to the border before and after the plant flowers. The range of colours, shapes and textures is greater than any other group of plants.

Good foliage plants

Acanthus	Foeniculum
Ajuga	Geranium
Alchmeilla	Grasses
Bergenia	Gunnera
Canna	Heuchera
Crocosmia	Hosta
Dicentra	Phormium
Epimedium	Rodgersia
Eryngium	Verbascum
Ferns	Zantedeschia

After flowering?

After flowering many perennials, hardy geraniums for example, can be cut to the ground and fresh leaves will appear, allowing them to remain as foliage plants for the rest of the season. Pulmonarias should be sheared over as soon as they have finished flowering and they will produce beautiful silver-splashed leaves. If they are left alone, then the foliage will look old and limp and will be an eyesore rather than an attraction.

▶ ▶ Also see: Herbaceous plants p.72-3, Seasonal plants and shrubs p.38-9

Colour?

As with shrubs, perennial plants have a great variety of leaf colours, some variegated, others with simple single colours. The colours should not be used at random but should be seen as part of the overall colour scheme of the border involving the flowers as well. Apart from green, there are very few colours that work as a block certainly care should be taken when using several variegated plants. However silver is an exception. Silver foliage blends well with a variety of flower colours, and the different textures and leaf shapes allows them to combine together to great effect. Soft pink flowers go especially well, but the combination of silver and bright yellow, although less frequently seen, is also very effective.

Silver foliage

Anaphalis
Artemisia
Celmisia
Centaurea 'Pulchra Major'
Cerastium tomentosum
Cynara cardunculus
Eryngium giganteum
Geranium renardii
Lychnis coronaria
Macleaya
Melianthus major
Onopordum
Romneya coulteri
Santolina
Stachys byzantina
Tanacetum haradjanii

Silver foliage

Above: To many gardeners the most interesting foliage plants are those with silver leaves. Although they are attractive in their own right, they also work well with a wide range of flower colours, both soft and brash. They are also valuable as 'linking' plants used to link colours that do not necessarily go well together. Silver plants nearly always like an open sunny position. They will languish and may eventually die in shade.

Fine foliage

Left: Foliage creates the framework of a garden. It acts as a foil for flowers and helps link together the various colours. In its own right it forms a decorative element, exhibiting many colours, textures and shapes. These hostas easily demonstrate this, beautifully setting off the hardy geranium as well as contributing colour and interesting shapes to the scene.

small trees and shrubs

Structure

Structure is an important element in the garden, especially during the winter when herbaceous plants have died back below ground. It is also of great significance during the summer months. As other plants come and go, it adds a sense of continuity. Trees and shrubs provide this. Evergreens, such as hollies, box and conifers, in particular, add a touch of permanence to a garden.

Most trees and shrubs have a limited flowering period and it is the foliage that provides most of the interest. Some shrubs can be boring when out of flower and have a hard time justifying their presence in a small garden. Choose shrubs that have a good shape and plenty of good foliage, and possibly autumn colour and berries as well to get the maximum from them. Many trees and shrubs, evergreens in particular, need very little by the way of attention.

Small is beautiful

Only choose small trees for a small garden. To a certain extent it can be argued that by the time the trees are big the planter will not be around to worry about them, but somebody will have to take them down. Besides, small trees are more in scale with the smaller garden, and since there are so many to choose from there is no need to go for vast oaks.

Autumn colour?

Get the most out of your trees and shrubs, look closely at what they offer and go for those that suit your needs. Autumn foliage is particularly desirable, the flaming reds and oranges are unbeatable as garden decoration.

Even better foliage?

There are a number of trees and shrubs that if coppiced produce larger and better coloured foliage. Most require cutting back in the spring, almost to the ground, choosing a place just above a bud. Several of the elders (Sambucus) respond very well to this, as does Rosa glauca. Eucalyptus gunnii is too big for a small garden when fully grown but it can be coppiced to not only keep it much smaller but also to produce better foliage.

 ▶▶ Also see: Seasonal plants and shrubs p.38-9

Topiary?

Although it is the underlying structure of branches and twigs that gives a tree or bush its shape, the foliage fills it out and turns it into a solid object. This is important where trees are used as silhouettes, tall conifers for example, but even more important where the tree or shrub has been specifically shaped as it is in topiary. Simple geometric shapes such as balls, cubes and cones can be created directly from the shrub by cutting the branches to shape as they grow, but more complicated shapes need to have a wooden or metal armature inside to which branches are trained and the outline sculpted as the shrub grows. Topiary is not difficult, but patience is required as the best material; box and yew are slow growing.

Small trees

Acer griseum
Acer japonicum
Acer pseudoplatanus 'Brilliantissima'
Amelanchier lamarckii
Betula pendula 'Youngii'
Cercis siliquastrum
Cornus
Crataegus
Gleditsa triacanthos 'Sunburst'
Ilex
Laburnum x waterei 'Vosii'
Magnolia stellata
Malus 'Profusion'
Malus sargentii
Prunus serrula
Prunus subhirtella autumnalis
Pyrus salicifolia 'Pendula'
Rhus typhina
Sorbus
Syringa

Suitable shrubs for topiary

Buxus sempervirens
Ilex
Laurus nobilis
Ligustrum ovalifolium
Taxus baccata

Evergreens?

Evergreen trees and shrubs are excellent at providing structure and interest all the year round in a garden. While a few conifers, such as leylandii, are very fast growing, many are extremely slow and are therefore ideal for the small garden. Most evergreens, including conifers need virtually no pruning or other attention. However too many evergreens, especially conifers can become a little boring, so mix them with other shrubs.

Easy maintenance
An evergreen border (above) not only provides year-round interest but also provides one that needs little maintenance. The shrubs need little pruning and their thick foliage creates a perfect ground cover to keep the weeds down. Tight-growing evergreens, such as box (left) and yew, are ideal subjects for creating topiary. Simple geometric shapes such as these spheres can be clipped without the need for internal formers.

retirement remedies

Carry on gardening

Not all gardeners are as active as they might like to be. Some are elderly and less able than they once were, while others have a disability which prevents them from gardening in the conventional manner. Gardening not only supplies an interest but also provides gentle exercise as well as the opportunity to get outside and do something other than simply sitting in the sun. Fortunately there are ways and means for people to continue to garden in one form or another, including creating miniature gardens in seed trays.

Safety?

Allied to the problem of moving around is the fact that it should be done safely. Surfaces should not be slippery and glass and water should be kept away from places where people move about.

What to do?

Once the problem of moving around the garden has been resolved then there is the question of what jobs can be comfortably carried out. As will be seen over the next few pages, there is a surprising amount. Some will be able to garden in the conventional manner, except tools will have to be adapted to make them able to be held more easily. Others will have to need the garden brought up to them so that it can be attended while sitting or even standing.

Scaling it down?

One of the secrets of limited gardening is to acknowledge ones' limitations and scale down the garden accordingly. Things like mowing lawns, and digging may be too strenuous, whereas tending a few raised beds with nothing more than a hand fork and trowel may well be possible. For others it may be necessary to scale down even further and create a miniature garden in a container that may be placed on a table or even a lap. This may be the answer, enabling gardening to be carried out in a much more limited way.

What plants?

Obviously plants that are unpleasant or difficult to handle are best avoided, thus prickly plants should be excluded and those that form large and cumbersome clumps. The partially sighted will enjoy those colours that stand out and are likely to have a preference for powerful scents.

Under cover?

The weather is not always kind to gardeners and the elderly may have difficulty scurrying for cover, so it is an idea to provide easily accessible shelter from sudden downpours. Similarly they may not want to be in the sun all the time, so shady places are also welcome, both to relax and to potter. During inclement weather, working in a greenhouse can be a pleasant occupation. Alternatively a conservatory attached to the house may be adapted as a greenhouse, providing the opportunity for all-year round gardening.

Gardening for the Blind?

There are many partially sighted and even blind gardeners. One of the keys to success for them is to be able to find their way around. The garden should be well laid out in a logical design and the different areas should be well flagged so that the gardener can easily find their own way around. Many of the tools are conventional, but things like measuring sticks should be marked with indentations rather than with a pencil.

Easy fruit
Climbing ladders is an occupation that the elderly or less able gardeners can contemplate. Fruit growers have bred trees of all types of fruit that can be easily picked from the ground, thus saving the necessity to climb or even stretch. It is worth searching these trees out and planting one or two as there is nothing quite like fruit picked freshly from the tree. In many cases the trees can be grown against walls or wire framework, but there are increasingly varieties that can be grown in containers which can even be reached from wheelchairs.

design and surfaces

Care must be taken with the design of the garden for the elderly and those with restricted abilities, difficult corners, steps and slippery surfaces should be eliminated and the flower-beds should be designed in such a way that they are accessible and easy to reach, even from a wheelchair.

Paths?

One of the most important aspects of designing a garden for the elderly is to make certain that access is easy and safe. Paths should be wide enough for a person with sticks or in a wheel chair to pass along them. The surface should be free from bumps or any edges that may cause them to trip, but on the other hand they should not be so smooth that they are slippery. A textured surface will allow a grip as well as preventing glare, which may well temporary dazzle or blind those looking at the ground as they walk. Brick paths are notorious for attracting very slippery algae and moss, Either they should be replaced or regularly treated with an algicide. Wooden surfaces can also be very slippery when wet. These should be avoided unless it is possible to improve the grip on them by cutting ridges in the surface. Attaching chicken wire is very effective, but it is only really suitable in this case for wheel chairs as the elderly could stumble as their shoes may well catch on the very rough surface.

Steady path
As people get older their risk from slipping or tripping up increases. Make certain that all paths are free from sudden unevenness, but at the same time having a roughened surface to prevent slipping. It should be well-drained so that there is no standing water or puddles. A contrasting colour along the edge will help to delineate the paths for the partially sighted. Avoid unnecessary curves or corners.

▶▶ Also see: Pathways p.94-5, Steps and stairways p.106-7

Stepping out

If possible replace steps with a gently sloping ramp, or at least give the ramp as an alternative. All steps should be flanked by sturdy handrails. These can also be used along the edge of terraces or difficult paths. It is important that the rails should inspire confidence so they should be well fixed and not rock or move. Wooden ones should be regularly inspected to make certain that they have not rotted and thus liable to sudden collapse.

Steps?

Steps should be eliminated if possible and replaced by a gentle slope. Even those elderly people that are not infirm will find manoeuvring wheelbarrows or mowing machines up steps an increasingly difficult task. Slopes or any other tricky areas should be lined with hand rails.

Access?

Access should also be wide enough for wheelchairs and people with sticks. This applies not only to gateways and archways, but also doorways to greenhouses and other buildings. Handles on doors and gates should be easy to use.

Glass?

Glass is potentially very dangerous. In greenhouses the gardener is usually kept away from the glass by the staging, but it may be necessary to put protection near the doors. Avoid putting paths alongside a greenhouse where there is the danger of falling on to it. A fence can help. Similarly, avoid using coldframes with glass lights. Use plastic or even polythene which, although not quite as effective as glass, is much safer.

tending the garden made easy

Gardening for the elderly is not all about safety, it is also about ways and means of looking after plants. One of the biggest problems is that the ground is a long way down, especially for somebody who cannot bend or kneel. The solution is to bring it closer in one way or another.

Reaching out
The elderly often have difficulty in gripping conventional tools. Life is made considerably easier by buying special tools with handles that have been adapted for easy use (right). Being able to work at a distance is another problem and, again, special tools can help. They can be purchased or made with extended handles (above) so that the user does not have to bend.

Tools?

The right tools are very important for the elderly and disabled. Some may like to make their own but there is an increasing number of tools becoming available from specialist shops. There are two aspects to choosing tools. One is that long handles prevent the need for bending or leaning forward. The other is that many people have increasing difficulty in gripping normal handles and need special handles that are easier to hold. Tools need not be expensive or complicated. A length of plastic water pipe provides a simple way of sowing seed from a wheelchair.

Cutting out the difficult jobs?

Attending plants is not too arduous but things like mowing the lawn and cutting hedges, become more difficult as the years pass. Sad as it is to see the lawn go, it may be time to consider altering the garden, so that the lawn is turned over to a paved area or perhaps to shrubs or ground-cover plants. Similarly, unless you can get help to cut hedges, then a fence or wall becomes an easier proposition. With a deal of foresight, a yew hedge planted well ahead of old age will be easier to tend as it only needs cutting once a year.

Raised beds?

Another way of making life easier is to bring the soil up to workable height. This involves some form of raised bed. The height and shape may vary depending on the person using it. Work from wheelchairs, for example is much easier if the bed is a raised one as this eliminates any bending down. The wheelchair can be brought alongside, or ever pushed up tight against it if there is a knee-hole or overhang all the way round. The raised beds can be built from brick or stone or they can be purchased especially made in plastic. ordinary chairs or stools can also be used with raised beds.

 ▶ ▶ Also see: Low maintenance p.10-11, Tool guide p.122-3

Within reach
Bringing the soil up to a workable height is one solution for those who have difficulty bending. Raised beds (left:) make tending plants much easier. It is possible to make special 'T' shaped beds so that a wheelchair can be manoeuvred under the top (like a table), bringing the work surface even closer. Fruit trees and shrubs (below) should be limited in height to provide easy access.

Over-reaching?

Not only is bending a problem for many gardeners, reaching, above the head or into the distance is also difficult. Fruit trees, for example, become impossible to climb or reach. However it is possible to use cordon fruit which grow at the right height for attending to from a standing position or from a wheel chair. Reaching forward too far can be eliminated by using narrow borders.

entrances and exits

Making an entrance

The entrance to a garden is usually already in existence when a house is bought and garden established and, therefore, many people do not give it a second thought. However, it pays to look carefully at both the entrance to the house and garden and also to the various entrances and exits between different areas of the garden.

First and last?

The entrance to a garden is one of the most important features as it sets the tone for the rest of the garden. It invariably provides the first impression that visitors will have of the garden. Similarly the exit is the last thing seen by visitors.

Setting the tone?

The type of entrance and the way that it is executed, therefore, set the tone of the garden. It should be in keeping with the style of the rest of the garden. A formal garden, needs a formal entrance, while a cottage garden, can have a much more relaxed approach.

Keeping the world at bay?

One must not forget that traditionally an entrance to a garden was the guardian of one's safety. It was there to allow entrance through the defenses that kept out animals and foe. While it is not usually quite so heavily fortified now, it still performs that basic function; it shuts out the outside world. However, this does not mean that entrances should be threatening, but they are still better if they look strong enough to be closed, even if they never are.

Beyond the threshold?

Nowadays the barriers around a garden are used more to keep out the eye than as a physical barricade. The entrance is the one place where the eye can look through and this is very important as the gateway is not only a physical entrance to a garden, but also a visual one. As you enter you get a glimpse of what lies beyond. In a good garden, this glimpse is tantalising and it draws you in.

Just looking?

As with so many aspects of garden design, it is a good thing simply to stand and stare. Stand outside any external or internal entrance and just look through it. Look to see whether it is enticing and whether it is representative of what lies beyond. Does the entrance reveal too much or too little. How can it be improved.

Improving the view?

Does the type of path and its condition make the right statement? Does it need changing or improving, does the view itself need enhancing in any way? Perhaps a focal point should be added to draw the eye, the direction of the path should be altered so that it moves enticingly out of view. If the gateway looks directly to the entrance of the house, does anything need to be done to improve the area around the door or even the door itself?

Getting inspiration?

Because the main entrance is usually on the road, it is possible to see plenty of examples and collect ideas simply by walking around a town or village. The exercise is a good one as you will see bad examples as well as good ones and will become aware of the pitfalls and so avoid things that either do not work or are out of keeping with what you want to create.

Picture perfect
A gateway can be a dramatic introduction to a garden. The archway serves several functions beside the obvious one of holding the gate up. As can be seen here they also act as a support for climbing plants such as roses, clematis and honeysuckle. They also frame the garden beyond, frequently creating an enticing image, drawing the visitor through to investigate.

driveways

Drive in
Driveways are a necessity that most gardeners could do without as they are large, often boring, and difficult to disguise. However it is possible to make them so that they are visually attractive as well as practical. They should be wide enough that people do not stand on the borders when getting out of cars and, if possible, have an interesting curving shape (right). Soften the edges with shrubs and other plants. If the drive is a straight, one with two strips of concrete or slabs (opposite) place low-growing plants along the middle.

Driveways are one of the most difficult things to get right in a garden. Unless they are on a grand scale, elegantly sweeping round to the front of a mansion, they are not particularly beautiful things. This is because in the main they are purely functional. They are used as somewhere to park the car, somewhere to load or get into the car, or as access to the garage. Frequently they have even less attractive qualities, such as somewhere to dump a load of sand or building bricks, or somewhere to store a caravan or boat. However, there are many ways to improve the appearance of a driveway.

A solid base?

A drive must be well built as it takes a heavy load. One that sags or has a broken surface is not only an eyesore but it also potentially dangerous. If there are any doubts about your capabilities, have it built professionally. It must have a solid foundation of rammed hardcore, topped with a layer of concrete and then finished with whichever surface you want.

Surfaces?

The concrete surface can be left as the final finish. This will look raw for some time, but will eventually tone down. It is the best surface if you intend to have sand dumped on it or if you use mix concrete on it as these will spoil any other surface.

Tarmac has a rather public-looking, bland quality about it, but once it weathers it has a certain 'softness'

about it. Normally it is black turning to grey, but it can be obtained in other colours and can have white chips rolled in to relieve the surface.

Gravel drives are very attractive both to the eye and to the ear as they produce a satisfying crunch under the wheels of a car. For drives they should have a solid foundation and should not be laid directly on the soil. Concrete is the best foundation. It should be sprayed with tar and a layer of gravel rolled into it. A thin loose layer can be laid on top to get the noise and typical wheel marks.

Brick or pavers are increasingly being used for drives. They produce an attractive, decorative surface. They must have a good surface under them.

Paving slabs can be used but, again, should be on a concrete base to prevent uneven subsidence. Various colours and patterns are available.

Welcoming scents?

It is difficult to disguise a drive. It can be edged with shrubs so that it is not visible from the rest of the garden, but for security reasons this might not be desirable. Herbaceous plants will make an attractive alternative. If possible, position a fragrant shrub or plant near the area where you stop the car as this will be a most 'welcome-home' smell after a day's work and, with luck, remove some of the tensions of the outside world.

Containing thugs?

An old-fashioned way of creating a drive that is not so overpowering as the all-over modern method, is to lay two strips of concrete where the wheels are to run. This leaves a rather awkward strip of earth down the middle, which can be left to grass or it can be used for flowering plants. There are a number of attractive low-growing plants that are too much like thugs to put in the open borders, where they swamp everything. Containment between the concrete strips is an ideal place for these as they can fight it out amongst themselves without interfering with more delicate plants. Acaena, pratia, ground elder and thyme are four such.

gates and porches

Suit the situation
Try and fit the gateway or porch to the style of garden or building. Both the gate (right) and the porch (far right) are rustic to suit their cottage-like situation. Choice of the right style and its interpretation is very important as gateways and porches are two things that visitors first notices, and they set the tone for what is to come.

Internal gateways
Although a heavy metal gate with solid brick piers (opposite) gives the impression of impregnable security it also acts as a welcoming entrance. It frames the view beyond and makes the visitor want to pass through to see what lies beyond. Even internal gateways, where security is not of prime concern, can be heavily constructed to advantage.

The visual impact of both gateways and porches is enormous. Neither are things which are usually bought 'off-the-peg' and so a great deal of thought needs to be put into what they should look like and how they can be made, even if someone else is employed to make them.

Simple gateways?

The simplest of gateways is just a hole in the hedge or fence. While this can work well for internal boundaries it is not very satisfactory for external boundaries. Next to this a wooden or metal gate is inserted into the fence or hedge without any frills. There is a great range of gates available, some simple other very ornate. Normally the gate is the same height as the fence or smaller if it is a high hedge. Make certain that the bases of the gate posts are buried deeply into the ground (at least 75cm/30in) and held firmly with concrete.

Archways?

A more complicated, but more interesting, way of creating a gateway is to introduce an arch. The archway can be a simple framework built from wood or metal, or it can be a solid object created from brick or even by letting the hedge grow up and over the gate. Gates in arches can be more complicated in design and are often tall.

Porches?

Porches are more of an architectural feature than a garden one, but often they are no more than a simple framework with climbers growing over them. These can be a similar construction to arches other parts of the garden, except that one side is attached to the building. Make certain that the porch is big enough if climbers are to be used as they will hang through the framework restricting the size of the entrance, and may possibly scratch people entering, if the structure is too small. Never add a porch that is out of keeping with the building.

Climbers?

Arches over gateways, apart from those constructed from hedging, are perfect for growing climbing plants. Roses are ideal but thornless varieties should be chosen if possible. Clematis make good companions to roses and between them provide a long period of flowering.

▶▶ Also see: Entrances and exits p.88-9, Arches and trellises p.66-7

pathways

On the road

Paths are an important aspect of garden design and should always be thought about very carefully. They not only provide the means of getting from one place to another with dry feet but also have a strong visual importance. There is a wide range of materials to suit all situations and taste.

Visual importance?

As well as carrying feet, paths tend to carry the eye. On entering a new area of garden the viewer automatically looks along the course of the path as it winds through borders, shrubs and other features. This has two implications. The first is that paths are always noticed and should therefore be well designed and constructed, using sympathetic materials. The second is that the path must lead somewhere visually as well as physically. It must lead to a focal point, a piece of sculpture or a specimen plant perhaps, or it should drift out of view round a corner, giving a sense of mystery and more to come.

Straight paths?

Think carefully where a path is to be placed. A path down the middle of the garden dissects into two halves. This may be convenient if you want rows of vegetables on either side, but it does very little from the aesthetic point of view. It is also impractical if you have a lawn spanning the garden as it will be split in two by the path. A path down one side has a practical ring to it, but although it may give access to the bottom of the garden, it does leaves a lot of the garden without direct access, to either see or tend what is there. Besides straight paths tend to be boring unless skillfully handled (a pergola or a series of arches will transform one), although if it is a path that is used a great deal then a straight one is the most convenient.

Meandering paths?

Paths that wander round a garden, tend to promote a leisurely wander, straight paths tend to draw the visitor on as quickly as possible. Paths that wind their way between borders make you feel as if you are right in the midst of the plants, and you ultimately feel much more involved with their growth.

Short cuts?

However, in certain circumstances it is often a good thing to avoid sharp angles in a path, particularly if there is not a fence or building within the angle. The reason for this is that human beings are prone to take the shortest route from A to B and inevitably people will take a short cut across the angle even if there is a bed or border there. This is particularly relevant in front gardens, where regular visitors such as paper boys, postmen and milkmen will always (quite naturally) try to reduce the amount of distance involved at each house. Make front paths as direct as possible from the front gate to the door. Any paths leading from it that are used purely to wander around the garden can be as convoluted as you like.

Materials?

There is a wide choice of material for use as garden paths. For much used paths, a hard surface, such as paving slabs, would be preferred. Paths that are used mainly for wandering along in summer can be of less durable material. Here, grass is one of the cheapest and the easiest option, although it will have to be frequently mowed and it can become muddy and worn in a wet climate. Gravel is softer than slabs of stone or concrete but it is more weather and wear-proof than grass. It also looks very good and makes a satisfying noise when walked on. The cheapest of all is a simple beaten-earth path as found in many old-fashioned cottages.

The way ahead

Pathways are an extremely important part of any garden. They are visual arteries as well as physical ones; they carry the eye as well as the feet. The nature and quality of a path should never be skimped. They can be made from a wide number of materials, paving slabs, seen here, being one of the easiest methods of achieving good results.

brick and stone

Brick
Although man-ufactured, brick is a natural material and the colour is usually based on earth-colours, working well in a garden situation where it should blend with soil and plants. Brick is very versatile and lends itself to the imagination as it can be used to create all manner of shapes and patterns.

One of the most durable materials is brick or alternatively those made from some sort of stone, including concrete. These are hard materials, both physically and visually and need to be handled carefully in a garden so that they complement the rest of the design. Plan carefully as a good path will last a long time.

Brick?
Brick paths are amongst the most beautiful. It is however important to get the colour and the pattern right and to ensure they are frost proof. Special pavers can be used but these are usually far more regular than bricks and do not produce the same feel. Bricks can be very slippery if they are used in a damp or shady position and should be scrubbed or treated with an algicide to keep them safe. Bricks can be laid on a concrete foundation, or, if the path is not too heavily used, be laid on rammed hardcore that has been blinded with sand. There are a number of traditional patterns that can be used.

Paving slabs?
Although they may not always look particularly elegant, paving slabs are very practical. The larger sizes are big enough to be laid onto rammed earth without necessarily laying a concrete foundation, as long as there is not too much heavy traffic. Another advantage is that they can be lifted and re-used, making it easy to redesign the garden. Genuine stone slabs are very expensive, but there are some good reproduction ones which have a textured surface. If you make your own it helps if the concrete is brushed over before it sets hard to remove some of the cement and to expose some of the small stones. This leaves an attractive texture. Natural coloured slabs tend to look best in paths, coloured ones often clash with the plants in the borders.

▶ ▶ Also see: Surfaces p.10-11, Steps and stairways p.106-7

Crazy paving
Pieces of irregular paving or stones are used to create a path with an informal, almost haphazard, look. Such paths feel friendly and are particularly good in cottage-style and other informal gardens. Match the stones well so that the gaps are not too large otherwise there will be large areas of cement showing. The edge can be irregular as here or lined with brick to finish it more neatly. Plants pouring over the edges make it look even more informal.

Mixed media?

Paving slabs can look a bit bleak at times. Mixing them with other materials makes a lot of difference to their appearance. A row of bricks on either side with the occasional transverse one lifts the look of the slabs completely. Mixing plain concrete slabs with those surfaced with large pebbles also makes an interesting contrast.

Crazy paving?

Crazy paving can be made from broken slabs of paving of varying size. It needs a firm base, either rammed hardcore topped with sand or a layer of concrete. Mixed colours can be effective if used well, particularly in designs for a Mediterranean type garden, but plain slabs tend to draw less attention to themselves.

Cobblestone?

Granite setts are expensive but they produce a beautiful path. A mass of them may be overpowering and mixing them with another media, such as gravel or slabs is ideal. Because they are uneven they can be a little uncomfortable to walk on. Large rounded pebbles can be used in the same way but these are decidedly uncomfortable if you have to walk a long way. They are best used for short distances or decoration.

Concrete?

Concrete makes a solid, practical path. Initially, the fresh concrete has a raw appearance but this will eventually weather to a much softer appearance which can look quite attractive. One disadvantage is that a lot of effort is needed to lift and re-lay fresh concrete, if you decide to move the path. A foundation of rammed hardcore is needed.

earth, wood and gravel

Earth, grass and gravel are much softer materials for paths than stone or brick, both to walk on and to look at, they are also, generally, the cheaper options. Softer materials also have the advantage over harder options in that they can be more easily re-laid in another direction.

Earth paths?

Earth paths are just that: earth. They are beaten hard and kept clear of weeds by the constant passage of feet. They are the traditional paths of cottage gardens and were very often supplemented by the addition of ash and cinders from the fire and occasional stones thrown out of the surrounding flower and vegetable beds. Over a time these all form a hard crust that prevents the path becoming muddy in wet weather. They are best for old-fashioned-style gardens or in more formal situations, for paths that are tucked away from sight.

Grass paths?

Grass paths are cheap to produce and are generally very good to look at, but they suffer from one big drawback and that is that they require mowing at frequent intervals. Unfortunately, a shaggy path can make the whole garden look untidy even if it is not. If you do not have time to mow the grass, at least clip the edges which makes a surprising difference to its appearance. Avoid using grass paths were there is heavy activity as the grass will wear thin in places. If necessary use a heavy-duty grass. Use a good quality grass or grass seed and make certain that all perennial weeds have been removed from the soil. Any weeds in the lawn will be constantly trying to spread into the borders, involving a lot of unnecessary work to remove them.

Wandering off
Loose material, such as gravel or small stones make an ideal path as they are dry and yet soft to walk on. Many make a crunching sound under the shoes which is not only pleasantly satisfying, but can also act as an early warning on security grounds. Gravel paths work best if they have some form of edging to prevent the stones working their way into the borders.

Gravel?

Gravel has much to offer despite it probably being the most expensive of the three options. It generally looks very attractive, especially after it has been just raked. Depending on the colour, and different areas provide gravels of different colours, the path will set the flowers and other plants off well. Maintenance consists of

▶▶ Also see: Garden floors p.108-9, Surfaces p.110-11

Softly, softly
Left: Chipped bark is one of the easiest and most instant paths to lay; just tip it from a bag. It is very soft under foot. However it is very informal looking and is best used where this type of situation prevails. It is probably most at home on paths through trees and shrubs where it creates a natural woodland feel.

Green paths
Far left: Grass is possibly the most natural of materials for paths as it is composed of living material. It has the disadvantage of needing to be cut and is not very good in wet weather and winter and can wear under heavy use. Having said that, it is very difficult to beat in terms of appearance, especially when the path continues naturally on from a lawn or other area of grass.

treating with weedkiller or weeding by hand to keep them clean and raking the path over. If the gravel has been laid on compacted earth, it is inevitable that some will work its way down into the soil and so it will be necessary to add a few bags more every so often. If possible line the edge of the path with a kerb or other edging so that the gravel does not wander into borders.

Wood chippings?
Wood chippings are becoming increasingly available and these make marvellous soft paths, especially through shrubs and trees. Lay the bark on compacted soil between lines of logs or wood edging. Over time the chippings will decompose and so it is necessary to replenish them when their cover wears thin.

stepping stones

Stepping out
For areas that only take light traffic, stepping stones can be ideal. They are practical in that they help keep the feet dry and yet at the same time they are visually exciting. Children love them. Any shape of stone can be used, either regular or irregular. Rounds of tree-trunk can also be used (far right) but they can become slippery in wet weather, especially in shady positions.

Paths are not always the appropriate solution for creating access. A solid path across a lawn or through a border, for example, might create too strong a visual line. Replacing it with a broken line of a series of stepping stones may well be the solution. Stepping stones can also be used where the access is of a more limited kind. For example, a series of stones could be used to provide firm access for anyone working in a flower border while visitors would be inclined to keep to the clearly defined main paths.

Stone stones?

Depending on the circumstances, stepping stones can either be regular or irregular in shape. In a formal garden, round or square stones or slabs would provide the right appearance, but stones seemingly randomly placed, such as to provide limited access to a flower bed, would be better to arrange in an irregular outline. If the stones are let into grass they should be sunk a little lower than the surface of the lawn so that the grass can be mown without hitting the stone.

Stone on stones?

Grass and borders are not the only places to use stepping stones. They can look extremely attractive crossing a large area of gravel or even sunk into an area of concrete to create a contrasting pattern.

Walking on water?

In the ground, stepping stones are more likely to be slabs rather than actual stones, but if used in water across a small pond or stream then they would be proper three-dimensional stones. These can look very attractive, however, they must be firmly planted and not rock or there may be a disaster. Be careful if the pond has a plastic or rubber liner as the stone may puncture it.

Wooden stones?

An attractive alternative to stone stepping stones is wood. The most usual form that this takes is with roundels cut from a felled tree trunk. These are sunk into the ground in exactly the same way as stones. They look more in keeping in areas where there are trees and shrubs. Because they are in contact with damp earth they could rot easily so it is a good idea to treat them with preservative before laying. Wood can be very slippery in wet weather or a damp position and if they are likely to be used in these conditions, then nailing some chicken wire over the surface will make it grip-fast without spoiling its appearance.

 ▶ ▶ Also see: Pathways p.94-5, Brick and stone p.96-7

Walking on water
Real stepping stones across water, over a pond or stream are always fun. They should be stable and not too rounded otherwise there is the risk of a ducking, even if the water is only ankle deep. Be careful if there are young children around as stepping stones over water will draw them like a magnet with possible unfortunate consequences if adults are not about.

slopes

On level ground?

Some gardeners regard a sloping garden as a nuisance, others welcome one as a blessing. The reluctance to accept them is usually because the gardener cannot face the initial amount of work and cost required to turn the slope to advantage. From a design point of view having a plot on several levels is a wonderful opportunity to create an interesting garden.

Flattening the garden?

One solution would be to flatten the whole garden, lowering one end and raising the other. The main advantage of a flat garden would be if the gardener were elderly or disabled and had difficulty with steps and slopes. Many vegetable gardeners would prefer a flat surface on which to work, but some of the best vegetable producers live on the sides of mountains, creating terraces in which to grow their produce. Unless infirmity necessitates a flat garden, go with it and utilise the slopes.

Slopes or terraces?

While it is not necessarily desirable to level the whole garden, one of the best ways of dealing with a slope is to flatten it out in sections or terraces, so that there are level areas for beds, lawns, and places to sit. These are interconnected with sloping paths and steps. Having said that, there is no reason why the garden should not simply be left as a slope and gardened as if it were flat. This would easily work if the slope is only a minor one, but if it begins to get steep the loose top soil will gradually work its way down the slope. Another disadvantage of a steep slope is that it is very tiring to work on it.

Holding back the slope?

If the slope is flattened into a series of terraces, then there must be a way of holding back the soil to prevent it all moving down the hill. The simplest way is to alter the garden from one continuous slope to a series of flat areas supported by much steeper slopes or banks. This, in effect is re-contouring the slope. Another, usually more attractive, way is to build a series of retaining walls. These can be left plain or used as a home for rock-loving plants.

Using contours?

Not all slopes are one-directional, they often move in different directions, or there may be promontories sticking out. Make use of these and contour the slope. It will look much more interesting than a series of parallel slopes.

Decking?

One way of dealing with a slope without having to move much earth is to use wooden decking built out over the slope. Hardwood is by far the best material, but if strapped for cash softwood can be used as long as it is treated with preservative and is well prepared to avoid splinters. Decking can be a perfect place for entertaining and relaxing.

Flowers in the bank
A bank of flowering plants is more likely to make a strong visual impact than the same flowers planted on flat ground. A garden on a slope can be much more interesting than a flat one, but on the other hand it can be very tiring for the elderly, especially when mowing or moving wheelbarrows.

Creating a slope?

There is no reason why terraces should not be created in a flat garden, certainly it will add interest to it. One way to do this is to build a patio that is raised above the surrounding garden. An alternative is to do the opposite and excavate out a sitting area that is lower than the surrounding beds. It need not be deep, even 15cm (6in) will be enough to emphasise the different areas. Another way of creating a variety of heights in the garden is to build a rock garden or to build an artificial slope with a small stream running down it.

terraces and retaining walls

Terraces may conjure up images of gardens clinging to the side of mountains, but even a modest slope can be terraced. Basically, it simply means flattening out certain areas of a slope using banks or retaining walls to compensate for the slope. A lot of effort may be involved but the rewards are tremendous.

Bank or wall?

Banks are cheaper and easier to construct than walls. In an informal design they work perfectly, although low ones are usually visually better and physically more stable than taller ones. Retaining walls are generally much more attractive and will fit in with most styles of garden. If planting holes are left in the brick or stone work then they can be decorated with plants.

Building walls?

Retaining walls may be holding back a great deal of weight and if there is any doubt in the gardener's mind as to his ability then it is safer to enlist the help of a professional builder. A low wall that is more decorative rather than supportive is well within the cap- abilities of most. Carefully work out the levels and redistribute the soil to achieve these. Be careful not to mix up the topsoil and the subsoil. Retaining walls will need good foundations. The wall itself can be built from stone, brick or concrete blocks, the last not being particularly attractive, but probably the cheapest. Slope the wall back slightly towards the terrace.

Drainage?

Water may well build up behind the wall so drainage pipes should be inserted at intervals. Alternatively, the vertical pointing between bricks or stones can be left out every so often. The drainage outlets should be at ground level on the lower slope side. Before filling in the gap between the wall and the slope, pour in a layer of rubble to help with the drainage. Preferably this should go right along the wall level with the drainage holes, but if there is not enough, a quantity round each hole will suffice.

Retaining walls
The expression 'retaining wall' can conjure up a bleak image of the reinforced concrete used in civil engineering projects. However, in the garden, they can be treated much more sympathetically as these two contrasting images illustrate. As well as levelling the ground, a retaining wall offers the opportunity for a decorative element that fits in with the style of the garden.

Backfilling?

The wall will be built a little way from the terrace so that there is work access to both sides. Once it is complete this gap should be filled in with soil to complete the terrace. Make certain that the top layer is top soil. If it is intended to plant along the top of the wall, it does no harm to fill the whole of the gap with topsoil.

Planting?

Some retaining walls, especially dry-stone walling, looks splendid with a few plants growing over them. Normally there are enough gaps in a dry stone wall to push in some compost and a plant, but gaps must be left in a cemented stone wall or a brick one. Be certain that the gaps do not weaken the wall. Sometimes it is possible to squash the rootball of a plant and then slide it in. Often it is easier to start from scratch, by blowing seed into a crevice or easing a rooted cutting (the roots wrapped in dampened tissue paper) into a crevice along with some compost.

Plants for walls

Aubrieta
Aurinia (Alyssum)
Armeria caespitosa
Campanula portenschlagiana
Erigeron mucronatus
Lewisia cotyledon
Phlox douglasii
Phlox subulata

Retaining steps

Steps can be built directly into a slope but can look clumsy if they are allowed simply to disappear into the earth on either side. A stepped retaining wall makes a much better finish. It can also be used for holding the plants back, preventing them from swamping the steps in such a way that might become dangerous.

steps and stairways

Rustic steps
Rustic steps
(right and centre)
have a wonderfully
romantic appeal
about them. In
spite of their casual
appearance they
should be well
constructed and
safely bedded into
the ground. They
are probably best
used for little-used
byways than as
regular paths as
they can become
dangerous in wet
weather and
during the winter.

Access between different levels is of course extremely important.
There is a wide range of both materials and styles varying from
the formal to the informal, like the entrance to a garden, steps tend
to attract the eye and invite the visitor to ascend, particularly if the
top is hidden from sight by a stunning array of plants.

Style?

The steps can be built into the bank
or they can be built freestanding in
front. Freestanding steps are really
best suited to formal gardens, but they
may be suitable if the retaining wall
is already in existence as it is far less
trouble to build the steps in front,
rather than cutting through the wall
to the bank. Straight stairways have
a formality about them, but those
curving away into the undergrowth
are far less formal.

Materials?

Bricks are attractive and adaptable,
and can be used for a range of styles.
Stone is very attractive and particularly
suitable in areas where it is the local
building material. Stone steps may be
formal or informal, concrete blocks are
not so attractive but are easy to use.
Paving slabs are very easy to use as
well as being relatively cheap; plain
ones may look a bit boring. Wood is
very attractive, but may become very
slippery, chicken wire nailed to the
surface will make them non-slip. Logs
and sleepers (railway ties) can be used
for the risers and the step filled with
gravel, small stones or bark. This
method is cheap and very attractive
for an informal setting.

▶ ▶ Also see: Garden floors p.108-9, Entrances and exits p.88-9

Planting steps?

The angularity of steps and stairways can be softened by growing plants on them. While this is a good idea and has a lot to recommend it, safety must be the first consideration and do not do anything that could cause people to trip or slip. Plants, ivy for example, can be grown along the risers of the steps and kept clipped back out of harms way. Softer plants, such as Erigeron mucronatus can be use to grow in cracks and crevices. Other plants can be allowed to encroach over the sides of the steps as long as they do not cover it completely or are in any way dangerous.

Handrails?

Handrails can look ugly but they may be necessary if elderly people are likely to visit the garden. With care they can be made to fit in with the style of the steps and not be too obtrusive.

Ramps and slopes?

It is sensible to include a few slopes in the overall design. These will not only be welcomed by those who have difficulties with steps, but also by the gardener when it comes to moving wheelbarrows and lawnmowers about.

Joint ownership
Steps can be softened and given a greater appeal if they are partially overgrown with plants (above and centre). However make certain that there is enough tread so they are safe to use. Steps that wind away to disappear through a haze of plants immediately excite the sense of adventure and draws the visitor upwards.

garden floors

Ground cover

One tends to think of the garden as simply being covered in earth, but a great deal of this is likely to be hidden beneath some other form of covering. Variation in surfaces makes the garden more interesting visually as well as having a practical purpose.

Purpose?

When considering the design of the garden and the surfaces that will be required, it is important to think about the purpose and uses of the garden. If the sole purpose is to grow plants, then the majority of the garden will be down to borders, on the other hand if you want areas to sit and relax or entertain in, then a mixture of paved patios and grassed lawns are going to be required. If there are children around then areas to play in will be important. They may well require hard surfaces to ride or skate on with softer, grass surfaces to play games on.

Hard or soft?

Garden surfaces are usually hard or soft. The former include paving slabs, concrete and bricks, the soft include grass and wood chippings. As a rule of thumb the hard surfaces are expensive to lay but cheap and easy to maintain. On the other hand, the softer surfaces are generally cheaper to lay in the first place but more expensive both in time and cost to maintain.

Patios?

Nearly every garden has a terrace or a patio at some point. Generally these are placed near the house, often immediately against it. This is convenient for bringing food and drinks outside, and has the advantage in that it acts as a visual link between the house and the garden. However, if this area is in permanent shade, then it may well be better placed elsewhere. Patios can appear stark and bare, with little character. This is usually because of the choice of surface or because it is not softened with plants. Avoid glaring white or pale yellow surfaces that reflect the sun back up into the eyes. Chose a surface that is textured or a soft, neutral colour. Plain concrete is very harsh when first laid but will weather down. Paving slabs are probably the cheapest and easiest option, but they are helped visually if they are not laid in serried ranks. Use varying sizes to create a patter, either formal or random and perhaps mix it with other material. Patios are usually used a great deal so make certain that they are laid flat, with the slightest of slopes to shed rainwater.

Plain or patterned?

One advantage of a hard surface is that it is possible to experiment with all kinds of textures and shapes. Paving slabs can be mixed with large pebbles or granite setts. Bricks can be used to create outlines or more solid areas. With imagination, mosaics made from whole or broken tiles can be incorporated. While it may seem to be something that ought to be installed as fast as possible, it is worth spending time looking at examples in books or visiting different gardens and those that are open to the public just collecting ideas.

Marginal options?

Do not forget the edges. These are so often overlooked and the area just peters out into the next. Patios often look better if they have a low wall around them, or at least a row of contrasting slabs or bricks. Loose material such as gravel and bark, needs to be retained not only physically but visually and some form of edging helps enormously. Even most lawns benefit by having a crisp edge (except in informal settings when they can bleed off under trees and shrubs, although this does lead to mowing difficulties).

Low maintenance
In the ultimate low maintenance garden, the soil is covered completely and all plants are grown in containers. Here a paved courtyard covers all available space. When choosing flooring, think of the purpose of the surface, how you will use it and how much time you will have to maintain it.

surfaces

There are a wide range of materials to choose from garden centres and builder's merchants and from time to time unusual materials may come to hand that can be used. Although cost may be the ultimate deciding factor, try to choose surfaces that are most relevant to your needs and the design of the garden. As a rough rule of thumb, grass goes with plants and hard surfaces with sitting areas and low-maintenance gardens.

Stylish solutions
In country gardens or open areas grass (right) seems an obvious choice. In the town, especially within an enclosed space another option (opposite) is to use flag stones near the house, complemented by wooden decking covering the rest of the available space.

Paving stones?

Paving slabs come in different materials, sizes and colour. The most expensive is real stone, but there are some good (and bad) reproductions. There are also those made from straight forward concrete. The varying sizes make it possible to produce random or geometric patterns. Some of the colours are a bit garish and should be used with discretion. Natural stone colours are usually the most sympathetic. Lay the slab on a hardcore base that has been covered with a layer of builder's sand. Bed them well down so that they do not move.

Brick?

There is a wide choice of brick types available. Avoid those that are not frost hardy as these will soon crumble. Special bricks for paving (pavers) are widely available, but these are often too regular and produce a rather regimented surface. House bricks are more sympathetic in a garden setting. Earth colours are usually the best choice, but in mixed media surfaces, rich coloured ones may blend in well. They are best laid on sand on a concrete base.

Concrete?

Used with discretion this can be an attractive material, but can also produce a vast wasteland if used badly. Brushing the surface just before it finally sets hard, removes some of the cement exposing the stones it. This can be a very attractive finish. Lay it all in one session or the joins and differing colours will show. It should be laid on a well prepared hardcore base.

Grass?

Grass is possibly the most natural surface for a garden. It looks good and is sympathetic to the surroundings. With the right choice of grass seed it can be very hard wearing. However grass does have a downside, in that it needs regular mowing, aerating and treatment to prevent weeds and moss. The ground should be well prepared and all perennial weeds removed or killed. It can be sown or laid with turf, the latter being more expensive but quicker to establish.

Woodchippings?

Woodchippings provide a soft surface, particularly suited to children's play areas. It is also a natural-looking surface amongst trees or shrubs. It is cheaper to buy by the lorry load if you need a lot (or share with a neighbour) rather than in individual sacks. It can be laid directly onto the surface, or on a layer of perforated horticultural polythene, which allows the rain water to pass through but stops weeds coming up.

Gravel?

Gravel is an attractive and relatively cheap material. It comes in various colours and the stones can vary in size. Avoid large pebbles, except for detailing, as they are uncomfortable to walk on. The gravel can be laid on compacted soil, or on perforated horticultural polythene which prevents weeds coming up. An edging is advisable to prevent gravel moving into the borders or lawns. It will need topping up from time to time as it works into the soil.

Decking?

Wooden decking is an attractive form of surface. It is particularly useful where the ground is uneven or sloping. Depending on the size and scale, it might be necessary to have it professionally designed as it can be a formidable structure. If possible it should be built from hardwood.

 ▶▶ Also see: Brick and stone p.96-7, Earth, wood and gravel p.98-9

disguising essentials

Consider the whole

A garden is a bit like the kitchen or the bathroom in the house, it can be well decorated but it is still a work-space and there are always bound to be a number of functional bits and pieces around that are not particularly elegant to look at. When designing the garden, the whole of the outside space around the house must be considered even if it is not used for growing plants. You cannot have a pair of dustbins standing on the patio and hope no-one will see them, even though you may be so used to their presence that you have long since ceased to notice them.

Avoiding the problem?

Most of the items that will need disguising are likely to be utilitarian. The aforesaid dustbins being an obvious example; they must be stored somewhere. To ensure new garden features do not look out of place, consider design carefully. A garage for example, can be designed and built in such a way that it is attractive and in no need for disguise. Similarly, garden sheds or greenhouses can be made very attractive in their own right.

Disguise?

However, many gardeners cannot afford to spend much on, say a garage, or they will have inherited one from the previous owner and not be able to afford to replace it. As we will see over the next pages there are several ways of hiding objects from view or transforming them into something much more attractive.

Service area?

Sometimes the area may well be connected with the garden, but it is more of a service area and is better kept out of sight. Rows of plants in pots, for example, or cutting frames and the like in an area devoted to propagation. The compost bins are rarely an attractive sight, although there is no reason why they should not be designed in such as way that they are.

Concentrate or diversify?

Depending on the shape and design of the garden, it might be an idea to concentrate all the eyesores in one spot and cordon off the whole area, or it might be better to scatter them around, with each disguised and thus less obvious. It may be that one side of the garden needs to be fenced off, and used as a storage area. Do not fence things off so well that there is no access. You will need to get to compost bins with garden rubbish, and access to a shed should not be too convoluted that it is difficult to get the mower or wheelbarrow out.

The house?

Not all houses are beautiful and in extreme circumstances the appearance of the garden, or the effect that you are trying to create might be compromised by the house itself. There may not be much, short of rebuilding that can be done, but it is surprising what a covering of creepers or climbers will do. The house need not be hidden, colourful window boxes will draw the eye away from the building itself.

What may need hiding?

Some objects may go unnoticed because of their familiarity. Think about the appearance of everyday objects such as dustbins, drains, washing lines, garden sheds and garages.

Pipe dreams

Drain pipes are not the most attractive of items, so why not hide them and make use of them at the same time. Here a golden hop (*Humulus lupulus* 'Aureus') is trained up such a pipe. It can be planted directly into the ground or grown in a pot.

hiding utilities

The time and effort spent in disguising services within the garden will be worth it for the overall appearance of the garden. It is possible to hide all manner of objects either by constructional or gardening skill, or both. Plants are a natural choice for concealment.

Out of sight
A fence will cover all kinds of eyesores and plants can be used to make the disguise complete. Plant climbers over the fence panels to soften their surface and outline. If it is a shed or garage that is being hidden then the climbers can be trained directly over its surface, using wires or trellising to hold the plants in position.

Fencing it off?
The simplest way is to fence off the offending objects. A panel fence will totally hide them from view, but frequently look as stark as the object they are covering. A fence that allows a partial view through it will not be so severe and will break up the outline of the eyesore sufficiently to disguise it.

Climbing over it?
A classic gardener's method of hiding an object is to grow a climbing plant over it. This can be over the fence or trellis that is placed in front of it, or it directly over the object. The latter can be aided by attaching trellis or wires to the wall of the shed or garage. Some plants are very vigorous and do a good job of hiding what is underneath.

A lick of paint?
A simple way to disguise something is to paint it. An oil tank, for example, painted green is more likely to blend into to the background than one painted red or white. On the other hand there is no reason why the most should not be made of a flat surface and a painted. This can be something unconnected with the garden, or it can be a vista of some sort, perhaps purporting to be another part of the garden.

Drawing the eye?
One way to hide something is to place something else nearby so that the eye goes to that rather than an eyesore. A pool and fountain instantly grabs the attention and the nearby shed is likely to be overlooked.

Getting rid of it?
A radical solution is to look carefully at your eyesore and see if it is really needed. A pile of rubbish can easily be moved and not allowed to re-accumulate. Is the caravan ever likely to be used again? If not why not dispose of it and rent one should the desire take you.

Vigorous climbers for hiding eyesores
Clematis montana
Clematis rehderiana
Clematis viticella
Fallopia baldschuanica
Hedera
Humulus
Hydrangea anomala petiolaris
Lonicera periclymen
Parthenocissus
Rosa
Vitis coignetiae

▶ ▶ Also see: Inner boundaries p.120-1

Cover-up
Manhole covers are
one of a gardener's
nightmares. They
are usually ugly,
cannot be removed
or permanently
covered up as
access might be
needed at any time.
One way of coping
with the situation
is to cover it with
a container of plants.
However, do not
make it too heavy
as it may need
to be moved. .

private space

Staying private

Unless you let the public in on a regular basis, a garden is usually a private space, much in the same way as a house is. Unfortunately, unlike a house the garden is not usually surrounded by solid walls and a roof and so your privacy is frequently invaded.

Physical intrusion?

Although noise and visual intrusion are often a nuisance, it is the physical intrusion of burglars and others which is the most distressing. A thick, thorny hedge can be a powerful deterrent, as anyone entering must then do so through one of the regular entrances, which are more easy to control. However, a tall hedge screens burglar from the public walking by, so it should not be too tall. Planting spiny plants under windows also acts as a deterrent. Pyracantha is prickly enough to deter most people. Avoid having large bushes near doorways or front paths, behind which people can lurk, discreetly light paths and doorways, possibly using 'magic' eyes that switch on the lights as soon someone approaches. The bottom of hedges should be kept thick to keep out unwanted animals (or, indeed, keep them if they are your own).

Visual intrusion?

Most people like their private lives to be private, even if they are not doing anything that is in the slightest discreditable. They do not like neighbours or passers-by peering into their garden and watching what they are doing. Hedges, fences and walls are the most effective barriers. Hedges are, in many ways the easiest and cheapest option, but they have to be regularly maintained, and the person on the other side of the hedge might not be too keen on cutting his side. He may also not be too keen if your hedge becomes enormous, cutting out sun and light from his garden. A tall fence or trellis, or a combination of both, with climbers on is a good alternative and usually not so vigorous and contentious as a hedge.

Hidyholes?

If it is not possible to put up tall barriers around the garden, it is possible to plant screens within the garden to deflect the gaze from without. These are good as they can also mask activities from neighbouring upstair windows, which usually peer over fences and hedges. These can be localised screens, around an area where people sunbathe or eat, for example. On the other hand the use of trees and shrubs may be much more extensive, perhaps playing a dominant part in the garden, or at least around the margins of the garden with a few clear areas for flower beds and entertaining activities left in the middle.

Noise?

Unfortunately, the problem of noise intrusion is increasing. Not much can be done about it, although thick, evergreen hedges can help. Again, entertaining within an inner sanctum, such as an arbour or an area surrounded by shrubs, helps to reduce the interference.

Smells?

Problems with smells and smoke from bonfires and barbecues are difficult to tackle except by recourse to local by-laws. Again, tall hedges and fences that deflect the flow of air that is carrying the smell or smoke will help, but turbulence inside the boundary will often bring it down again. As with windbreaks, a double hedge, one set at a short distance from the other will help prevent this, but this is usually not a practical method if the garden is small and the nuisance only occasional. Using strongly scented shrubs and perennial plants in the garden can help to counteract the smells wafting over the hedge.

Country retreat
Secret hideaways are always worth creating. It allows a place for peace and tranquillity in a busy world. In this arbour, the encroaching plants create a womb-like retreat where a person can be very private. As well as sitting areas, similar private spaces can be created for sun bathing or eating meals.

outer boundaries

Dividing lines
The easiest form of outer boundary to create is a fence. Like most things in the garden there is no reason why the gardener should conform to other people's ideas. Create your own space, a horizontally boarded fence (above) has been decorated with odd bits of ironwork, creating an informal look. The painted picket-style fence, (opposite) has a much more formal look about it which fits perfectly with the clear-cut design of the garden and house.

Most gardens automatically come with some form of outer boundary even if it is only a piece of wire stretched between posts, but they are not always satisfactory both in terms of fitting in with the design of the garden and acting as a satisfactory boundary.

Why outer boundaries?

There are several reasons why attention should be paid to the outer boundaries of the garden. Firstly, there are the aspects of security and privacy already mentioned in previous pages. But there are also other reasons, more connected with the visual design of the garden. A good hedge, fence or wall should act as a perfect backdrop to borders or planting within the garden. A dark green hedge, for example, usually sets off the colours of flowers perfectly. They look much more striking than if they have nothing behind them. A fence or wall can be used to house plants or other decorations. Climbing plants, rose or clematis, look good in these situations and make a perfect edge to a garden. The wall or fence can also be decorated with window boxes, plaques, water-spouts, mosaics or in a number of other interesting ways. In other words, the boundary is part of the decorative effect of the garden and not just simply something to keep the neighbours out.

What to use?

Walls can be beautiful, but are very expensive, to be of any value as an outer boundary they must be reasonably high. The choice of colour of the brick or stone is very important. Concrete blocks are an alternative, but far less attractive. Fences come in all shapes and sizes, from a simple post and rail to solid lapboard. Some are only a token boundary and present no barrier against physical or visual intrusion, and are not particularly good at supporting plants. Picket fences and wattle hurdles, however can be very attractive.

Trellising is excellent for supporting plants but rather see-through and so better used for internal boundaries. It can be used effectively to extend the height of fences or walls.

Evergreen hedges make excellent anti-neighbour hedges as they are usually impenetrable both physically and visually. Yew is slow-growing but only requires cutting once a year. Leylandii roars away but forgets to stop, and requires frequent cutting or it gets out of control and is a frequent cause of disputes with neighbours.

Deciduous hedges are generally not such a soil boundary as evergreens, although they are usually just as effective. They are faster-growing than yew and most need at least two trims a year. Most are see-though in winter, although, beech and hornbeam generally hold onto their dead leaves.

 ▶ ▶ Also see: Entrances and exits p.88-9, Safety and security p.32-3

inner boundaries

Informal hurdles
Country hurdles made from hazel or willow make ideal internal screens. Their rustic quality makes them particularly useful for informal situations although they can be used in more formal positions where a contrast that is not too extreme is required. However, such hurdles are not a permanent solution as they will deteriorate after a few years.

To many gardeners the term inner boundaries may not seem to make much sense, but here it is used to refer to any form of screen or barrier that is used within the garden. These barriers may be used to screen or delineate different areas of the garden, or simply as a means of supporting climbing plants. A garden broken down into different areas or smaller gardens is always much more interesting than one where everything can be taken in with one glance. Inner boundaries help to create these. They can also be used for screening eyesores within your own garden.

Trellis?

Trellising is a gift for the gardener. It is an ideal barrier between different parts of the garden as it effectively blocks off one part from another, yet allows tantalising glimpses of what lies beyond. It is not as solid as the screen that is presented to the outside world. It is ideal for supporting climbers of all types. A flat garden can be boring, but trellising helps to create a vertical element that breaks up the garden. Of course, much trellising is attractive in its own right and can be used unadorned. There are many different shapes and patterns, and it is worth exploring the options before finally deciding what will suit your particular garden design.

Dwarf hedging

Buxus sempervirens 'Suffruticosa'
Lavandula angustifolia
Santolina chamaecyparis
Teucrium chamaedrys

Walls?

Walls within a small garden can look too solid, making the garden seem even smaller, but low walls definitely have a place, especially marking off one area of activity from another. The margins of a patio, for example, frequently benefit from having such a positive edge. Retaining walls are a form of barrier, marking off one level from another.

Hedges?

Tall hedges, like walls, can be too dominant a feature within a small garden, unless handled carefully. They can form too heavy a barrier. However, they are ideal for screening off utility areas if you want to avoid dustbins or compost boxes from being seen. Yew is the most attractive material for internal hedges, if you have the patience (a good yew hedge takes five to six years to mature).

▶ ▶ Also see: Arches and trellises p.104-5, Garden deceits p.64-5

Low barriers?

Hedges and walls do not have to be tall within a garden. Low box hedges, for example are excellent for breaking up the garden into compartments or smaller gardens. A fascinating use of dwarf hedges is to create a parterre or knot garden, where the hedges are arranged in a decorative pattern, often resembling a knot – the spaces between them being filled with colourful plants. As long as they are not too elaborate these can easily be created in a small garden. A potager can be created in a similar way, filling the small beds with vegetables and herbs for the kitchen.

Incidental boundaries?

Some forms of boundaries might not be considered as such, but they none-the-less form a dividing line between areas. A path, for example can form a simple boundary between flower borders and vegetable beds. A circle of different coloured bricks on a patio may mark out the space used for a round table, or be used for a particular activity. Visual markers add to the interest of a garden.

Vertical space

Space is often precious in the small garden and use should be made of every scrap of it. If internal barriers or screens are required then the use of trellising allows the inclusion of climbing plants. This not only allows the gardener to fit in more plants, but it makes the garden more three-dimensional, the space becomes more alive.

tool guide

A good set of tools are invaluable to a gardener. The right tool for the job will save a lot of time and effort. However, it is possible to garden successfully with only a few tools. One problem for the small gardener is that the more tools you have, the more space you will need to store them.

Quality?

Always buy the best you can afford. Cheap tools often bend or corrode very easily. They also lose any sharp edge they have very quickly. Old tools can often be found that have been made of excellent quality steel and these are frequently better than their modern equivalents. With modern tools, stainless steel is generally better than ordinary steel, although a lot more expensive.

Basic tool kit

Bucket
Fork
Garden line
Gloves
Hand fork
Hoe
Pruning saw
Rake
Secateurs
Shears
Spade
Trowel
Watering can

Extra tools?

The following tools are desirable but not essential as most jobs can be achieved with the basic tools.

Cultivator
Dibber
Hosepipe
Lawn edgers
Long-arm tree pruners
Loppers
Range of hoes
Sprinklers

Basic equipment?

Hedge trimmer
Lawn mower
Wheelbarrow

Extra equipment?

The following are useful but far from essential. Remember that equipment takes up a lot of storage space and requires maintenance to run properly.

Chainsaw
Lawn aerator
Lawn fertiliser spreader
Leaf sweepers
Rotavator or mechanical cultivator
Shredder/Strimmer

Storage?

Tools and equipment should have proper storage; they should not be left lying around in the garden. If there is enough space in a garage then this is ideal. Most tools can be hung from the wall, thus taking up very little space. Equipment, on the other hand, generally takes up floor space. It may be necessary to buy or build a shed to store the tools. This could have a workbench in it for potting and other activities.

Maintenance?

Clean all tools and equipment after use. Remove all soil and plant remains, such as leaves and sap and lightly oil the metal surfaces to prevent them rusting. Take particular care at the end of autumn when using things for the last time. All machinery should be maintained and sharpened at least once a year by a professional unless you able to do it yourself.

glossary

aerating Spiking a compacted lawn to allow air to penetrate to the roots.

alpines Theoretically plants from alpine regions, but applies to all plants grown on rock gardens, and alpine houses.

annuals Plants that germinate, flower, seed and die, all within the current year.

arbour A cave-like structure covered with climbers or made from shrubs. Usually contains seating and sometimes a table.

bare-rooted Plants are thus described if they are dug up from a nursery bed and sold without soil round their roots.

bedding plants Annual and tender perennial plants that are used for mass displays.

biennials Plants that germinate in their first year and flower, seed and die in their second.

biological control A method of controlling pests by introducing animal predators that eat or live off them.

blind (1) Flowering plants that produce buds that never open.
(2) Covering hardcore or rubble with a layer of builder's sand.

bog garden A border or area of the garden that never dries out and in which moisture-loving plants are grown.

bract A leaf-like appendage that appears just below a flower or forms part of the flower head.

broadcasting A method of sowing seed where the seed is scattered evenly across a surface rather than in rows.

calcareous Alkaline soil containing chalk or lime.

capillary matting A form of matting used in greenhouses that absorbs water from a reservoir and then supplies it to the plants through the bottom of the pots.

catch crop An intermediate crop of vegetables that utilises temporarily vacant ground.

cascade A stream that runs down a series of waterfalls.

Chinoiserie Design in a Chinese style.

clay Heavy sticky soil that needs to be 'improved' before it can be used successfully for gardening.

cloche A small movable frame that is covered in glass or polythene and used as a temporary cover for plants, especially vegetables.

climber A plant that climbs through other plants or up walls, fences and trellises.

clone A plant that has been vegetatively propagated and is identical to its parent.

coir An alternative to peat made from coconut fibre.

cold frame A miniature greenhouse that serves many of the same functions, except that it is low to the ground and thus cannot accommodate the gardener.

companion planting The use of plants that protect one another from pests and diseases.

compost (1) A special composition of soil used for growing plants in pots and containers. (2) The rotted remains of organic material that is waste from the garden and kitchen.

concrete A mixture of cement and small stones. It is extremely hard and durable.

container Any pot or other vessel for holding plants.

cordon A method of growing low fruit trees that consist basically of a single stem and are usually tied into wirework at an angle.

cottage garden A traditional garden found especially in rural areas, where the design was usually decidedly informal.

crazy paving Paving consisting of broken slabs or stones, arranged in a random order.

cultivar A distinct form of a particular species of plant.

cuttings Pieces of stem or root that are put into compost so that they produce roots and eventually become a new plant.

dead heading Removal of flower heads as they die.

deciduous Plants that lose their leaves during the winter.

decking A constructed wooden surface used as a patio.

division A method of propagating plants by breaking them up into small pieces.

drawn A plant that has become stretched and over-tall due to its searching for light.

dry stone wall A stone wall that is built without any mortar or cement.

edging The built-up edge of a lawn or path, laid either to visually or physically contain it.

ericaceous compost Special compost suitable for lime-hating plants such as rhododendrons and heathers.

espalier A form of training small trees, usually fruiting, against a wall or wires. It generally consists of a main stem with horizontal branches trained along the wires.

evergreen Plants that do not lose their leaves during the winter.

fan A form of training small trees, usually fruiting, against a wall or wires. The branches radiate from a the trunk in the form of a fan.

fasciation A malformation of a plant where the stems or flowers become fused together giving a strap-like appearance. It cannot be transmitted to other plants.

fastigiate A plant that grows like a slender column, upright.

fertiliser A powdered, pelletted or liquid nutrient supplement.

foliage Leaves.

foliar feeding A fertiliser that is applied in liquid form to the leaves of a plant through which it is absorbed.

fungicide A chemical applied to plants to control fungal diseases.

gazebo A form of open summerhouse, usually with a view.

germination The development of a seed into a small plant or seedling.

graft The physical union of two plants to form a new one.

gravel Small stones either water worn to size or made by crushing larger stones.

ground cover Plants or any material that covers that ground to suppress weeds and prevent evaporation of moisture.

growing bag Bags filled with compost into which plants can be directly planted.

half-hardy Tender plants (usually annuals) that will not stand a frost.

hardcore Stones or builders rubble used as a foundation.

hardening off The process by which seedlings are weaned from a warm indoor atmosphere to an outdoor one ready for planting out.

hardy Capable of withstanding frosts.

herbaceous Strictly speaking plants that die back to the ground in the winter, but used loosely to refer to any non-woody perennial plant.

herbicide Chemicals for killing plants, in particular weeds.

humidity Moisture content of the air.

inflorescence Flower head.

inorganic Material that does not derive from animals or vegetation. Strictly speaking substances that do not include carbon.

insecticide Chemicals used to kill insects.

kitchen garden Vegetable and herb garden.

knot garden A pattern of low hedges, often filled with colourful bedding or other plants.

lawn An area of grass that is kept relatively short.

leach The process by which nutrients and minerals are washed from the soil by constant rain or watering.

leaf mould Rotted and rotting leaves.

lime Forms of chalk and limestone that are added to the soil to increase its alkalinity.

loam A mixture of clay, sand and organic material forming a good, workable soil.

manure Bulky material, usually animal but can also be plant, used to feed and condition the soil.

maze A series of paths or passages between hedges that form an intricate pattern to the centre and exit, which are obscured.

micro-climate The local weather pattern.

moisture-retentive soil Soil containing organic material that retains sufficient moisture for plants' needs, but not enough to become waterlogged.

mulch A layer of organic or inert material that is laid over beds to suppress weeds and help preserve moisture.

nursery bed A bed for growing on plants until they are big enough to be planted in their final positions.

organic material Material that derives from animal or plant waste.

parterre A series of low hedges forming a pattern, often complicated, the centres of which may be filled with colourful plants.

patio A paved area, often adjacent to the house, mainly used for sitting and entertaining.

pavers Bricks specially made for use in paths, drives and patios.

perennial (1) Comes up every year. (2) Non-woody plants that continue from one year to the next, although they may die back for the winter.

pergola A series of arches covering a walkway, which are often covered with climbing plants.

pesticide A chemical for killing insect pests.

pH The scale against which the acidity/alkalinity of the soil is measured. pH6.6-7.3 is neutral, below is acid and above is alkaline. Plant growth requires between 5.5 and 7.5, 6.5 is optimum.

potager A vegetable and herb garden, often decorative in its design.

pruning The removal of branches and shoots from plants to improve their shape, health or performance.

raised beds Beds raised above the surface of the surrounding area, enclosed in low brick, stone, block or wooden walls.

reversion The changing back of variegated foliage to its normal green form.

rock plants Theoretically plants from alpine regions, but applies to all plants grown on rock gardens, and alpine houses.

rockery A garden or bed built with stone and well-drained soil to provide a natural-looking home for alpine plants.

rotation The process of changing the position of specific crops around the vegetable garden on a three or four year basis.

scree A form of very free-draining rock garden consisting mainly of stone that emulates mountain screes.

shrubbery A border devoted entirely to the growth of shrubs.

soak-away A deep hole loosely filled with rubble into which drains bring surface water, so that it can slowly soak away rather than remaining in the surrounding soil.

soil conditioner Organic material that improves the structure and nutritional value of the soil.

sprinkler A device for automatically spraying water over a large area in the garden.

staging The benching in a greenhouse on which the pots of plants are kept.

staking The supporting of plants using stakes, hoops or some other device.

standard A form of ornamental or fruit bush that is grown on the top of a single long stem.

subsoil The soil below the fertile topsoil.

sucker A stem that appears from underground next to a plant.

sunken garden A special part of the of garden that is deliberately sunken below the surrounding area.

terrace (1) A patio. (2) A level piece of ground created on a slope.

tilth The texture of the soil when dug and broken down.

topsoil The fertile top layer of soil.

trellis A wooden screen of criss-cross slats used to support plants, either free-standing or attached to a wall.

trompe-l'oeil A device, usually a painting, that deceives the eye.

trough A stone or cement container for housing a collection of small alpine plants.

underplanting The planting of plants under other, taller ones.

variegated Foliage (but sometimes also flowers) that exhibit more than one colour.

vegetative propagation Non-seed methods of propagation using a part of the original plant such as in taking cuttings or by division.

wattle Pliable stems, usually willow or hazel, woven into panels.

weedkiller A chemical used for killing weeds.

wigwam A conical structure of sticks or poles for growing climbing plants.

windbreak Shrubs or netting sited to slow down the wind.

index

acknowledgements

The publishers wish to thank the following organisations for their kind permission to reproduce the photographs in this book:

Clive Nichols Photography *front cover bottom right,* **12** *left,* **13** *bottom left,* **121** *top right,* /designer Richard Coward **4** *top right,* **50-51** *centre left,* /designer Dennis Fairweather **52-53** *centre right,* /Lisette Pleasance *front cover bottom left,* /Old Rectory, Northants **87** *bottom,* /designer Roger Platts **7** *bottom,* /Vic Shanley **105** *top,* /designer Stephen Woodhams *front cover top left.*

Elizabeth Whiting Associates 23 *top right,* /Andrea V. Einsiedel/designer R. Abel **4** *centre left,* **24,** /Michael Dunne **29** *top centre,* /A.V. Einsiedel **16,** /Di Lewis **13** *top centre left,* /Spike Powell/designers J&N Kent **18-19** *centre.*

Garden Picture Library/David Askham **108,** /Lynne Brotchie **4** *centre right,* **15** *bottom,* **47** *top right,* /Chris Burrows **70-71** *centre left,* /Bob Challinor **120-121** *centre,* /David England **44-45** *centre right,* **74** *centre,* /Ron Evans **79** *top right,* /John Glover *insert p.***2** *top left, insert p.***2** *top right,* **41** *top right,* **71** *top right,* **75** *top centre,* **112,** /Jaqui Hurst **106-107** *centre,* /Roger Hyan **50** *top left,* / Lamontagne **80** *top,* **120** *bottom left,* /Mayer/Le Scanff *insert p.***4** *top right,* **82,** /Zara McCalmont **56** *top right,* /John Miller **67** *top right,* /John Neubauer **118** *top centre,* /Clive Nichols **32** *top right,* **71** *centre right,* /Marie O'Hara **28** *top left,* **34-35** *centre,* **40-41** *centre,* /Jerry Pavia **78** *centre left,* **106** *top left,* **107** *top right,* /Howard Rice **10,** **27** *top right,* **39** *top right,* **75** *bottom centre,* **98-99** *top centre left,* /Gary Rogers **101** *centre left,* /John Ferro Sims **4** *bottom left,* **68,** /JS. Sira *insert* p.**3** *topleft,* **36,** **41** *centre right,* **44** *top left,* **44** *bottom left,* **48,** **100** *left,* /Freidrich Strauss **21** *left,* /Ron Sutherland **32** *top left,* **92** *top left,* **98** *bottom left,* /Juliette Wade **92** *top right,* /Steven Wooster **18** *bottom left,* **87** *top.*

Garden & Wildlife Matters 22-23 *centre,* /Zooid Pictures **34** *top.*

Gardening Which? 86 *top,* **86** *bottom.* John Glover *front cover top right,* **4** *top centre,* **13** *centre centre right,* **13** *top left,* **26-27** *centre,* **58** *left,* **78-79** *centre right,* **92-93** *centre right,* **102,** **104** *right,* /Burford House, Tenbury **96-97** *top centre right,* /designer A. Titchmarsh **4** *centre,* /designer K. Georgi **84-85** *top centre right,* /Great Dixter Garden **58-59** *centre,* /Ladywood Hants **116,** /designer P. McCann *back endpaper, front endpaper,* **15** *top,* /designer M. Smith *insert* **3** *top right,* **38,** /The Dillon Garden **47** *left,* /designer A. Titchmarsh **13** *top right,* **21** *top right,* /designer M. Walker **63** *centre,* / designer Geoffrey Whiten **4** *top left,* **54,** /Woking Borough Council **59** *top right.*

Harpur Garden Library Jerry Harpur/designer Robert Chittock, USA **19** *top right,* **97** *bottom centre,* /designer Jean M. Clark, Suffolk **9,** /designer Judith Sharpe, London **14** *left,* /designer Barbara Thomas, USA **64-65** *centre right,* /designer Bruce Kelly, USA **88,** /designer Christopher Masson, London **62** *top right,* /designer Edwina von Gal, USA **118-119** *centre right,* /designer Julie Toll, Herts **114** *left,* /designer Mark Rumary, Yoxford, Suffolk **94,** /designer Michael Balston, Wiltshire **34** *bottom,* /designer Simon Fraser, Teddington, Middx **111,** /designer Vernon Straton **56-57** *centre right,* /Dr. Christopher Grey-Wilson, Suffolk **4** *bottom centre,* **64** *top centre,* /Franchesca Watson, RSA **96** *centre left,* /Fuddlers Hall, Essex **66-67** *top centre,* /Jenkyn Place, Hampshire **72** *top left,* /Little Malvern Court, Hereford & Worcs. **81** *centre,* /Mrs K. Chattaway, Essex **81** *top,* /Oehme & Van Sweden, USA **52** *top left,* /Park Farm, Great Waltham, Essex **90** *top right,* /Sheila Chapman, Essex **110** *right,* /The Priory, Kemerton, Hereford & Worcs **72-73** *centre right,* Marcus Harpur/designer Andy Rees, Bucks **100** *right,* /designer Fiona Lawrenson, RHS Chelsea **1997 4** *bottom right,* **60.** Andrew Lawson **3** *centre,* **30,** **33** *top centre,* **76,** **99** *top right,* **104** *left,* /York Gate, Leeds **23** *centre right.*

Harry Smith Collection 22 *left,* **84** *bottom,* **91,** **114-115** *centre right,* **122** *right,* **122** *left,* **123.**

Reed Consumer Books Ltd./Andrew Lawson *front cover centre left,* **39** *bottom right, insert* p.**5** *centre,* /Steve Wooster *back cover centre,* **20** *top,* /Polly Wreford *back cover right,* /Neil Holmes **52** *bottom left,* /Jerry Harpur *insert background.*

Robert Harding Picture Library 46 *top right,* **51** *top right,* /Philip Craven **42,** /Family Circle/photographer Debbie Patterson *back cover left,* /Homes & Gardens IPC Magazines LTD/Polly Wreford *insert* p.**4** *top left,* **28** *top right,* /Simon Upton **7** *top.*